C. C Stewart

The scriptural Form of Church Government

C. C Stewart

The scriptural Form of Church Government

ISBN/EAN: 9783743330450

Manufactured in Europe, USA, Canada, Australia, Japa

Cover: Foto ©ninafisch / pixelio.de

Manufactured and distributed by brebook publishing software (www.brebook.com)

C. C Stewart

The scriptural Form of Church Government

C. C Stewart

The scriptural Form of Church Government

THE SCRIPTURAL FORM

OF

Church Government.

BY THE
Rev. C. C. Stewart, M.A.,
OWEN SOUND, ONTARIO.

"Rax me that Bible"—
                    JOHN ERSKINE.

SECOND EDITION.

TORONTO : JAMES CAMPBELL & SON.
NEW YORK :—THOMAS NELSON AND SONS.
EDINBURGH :—W. OLIPHANT AND CO.
LONDON :—J. NISBET AND CO.

MDCCCLXXII.

Entered according to the Act of the Parliament of Canada, in the year one thousand eight hundred and seventy-one, by REV. C. C. STEWART, *in the office of the Minister of Agriculture.*

PREFACE.

THE author of this little work is well aware that many men of far greater erudition and ability have preceded him in the field into which he has entered as a labourer, and have left behind them great and enduring monuments of their toil and skill. But notwithstanding all that they and others of less note have done, he could find no book, when he was a student, suited to his case. Some were so elaborate that he could not possibly find time to read them; others only took up a particular part of the subject such as, for example, the eldership; while a third was controversial, and contained a great deal that was personal and only of local interest, and, moreover, left unnoticed some of the most important questions. His difficulty was also felt by others, particularly by students and Bible-class teachers, and by all who were asked, as was frequently the case, for some book on the subject which gave, in as small compass as possible, as full a view of all the various questions of Church Government as is necessary to thoroughly ground one in the whole subject. Despairing of ever finding such a book, the author set to work to study the whole subject for himself, taking the Bible as his sole authority, while he availed himself of the help of all such works as were within his reach to throw light upon its teaching, that he might be able to produce something of the kind himself, and this book now offered to the public is the result of his labours.

He does not claim for it originality, but it has been his aim to set what he has been able to gather in a light so clear, that the most indolent could not complain of tediousness; the most stupid, of obscurity; nor the busiest, most energetic and clever, that their minds were not exercised, or that they were detained too long through diffuseness. Whether he has succeeded in gaining what he strove for, he leaves it for the public to say, to whom he now sends forth this, his humble attempt to make the path of knowledge, in as far as one very important subject is concerned, plainer and easier for all who come after him.

C. C. S.

OWEN SOUND,
    August, 1871.

THE SCRIPTURAL FORM

OF

CHURCH GOVERNMENT.

THE THESIS.

IN the following propositions, we may sum up all that we have to say on our subject:—

I. THE LORD JESUS CHRIST, SOLE KING AND HEAD OF THE CHURCH, HAS GIVEN OFFICERS BOTH FOR THE ESTABLISHMENT OF A COMPLETE SYSTEM OF CHURCH GOVERNMENT, AND ALSO FOR THE CARRYING OUT OF THAT SYSTEM.

II. HE HAS NOT LEFT IT TO ANY MAN OR BODY OF MEN TO DEVISE WHAT SCHEME THEY MAY SEE FIT; THE ONE HE HAS GIVEN IS FOR ALL; AND NO ONE HAS A RIGHT TO ADD TO IT, OR TO TAKE FROM IT.

CONTENTS.

CHAPTER I.

Shows who constitute the Church, and whence her prerogatives arise; explains how she comes to be divided into denominations, and what denominational differences amount to; and combats the errors of the Romanists, High Churchmen, and Plymouth Brethren, as to what is meant by "The Church," 11–31

CHAPTER II.

Proves that the Head of the Church, Jesus Christ, has given her a Ministry; vindicates the practice of those denominations which have a Ministry distinct from the private members of the Church; and exposes the unsoundness of the teaching of the Plymouth Brethren on this subject, ... 32–45

CHAPTER III.

Inquires as to the officers of which the Ministry is composed; finds that they are all of one order; reviews the arguments of the Prelatists, especially of the Episcopalians, and shows that their position is unscriptural, . 46–83

CHAPTER IV.

Treats of the officers mentioned in Paul's list by the name of Governments; shows that they are officers who rule in conjunction with the ministers of the Word, and, like the ministers, are elders; criticises the positions of Dr. Campbell, and justifies the theory of the Presbyterian Church, ... 84–98

CHAPTER V.

Brings forward the Scriptural grounds for the office of *deacon;* shows what are the duties of this office; proves from Hooker's admission, as well as from Scripture, that it is by the authority of Prelatic Churches alone that deacons are made ministers of the Word; and clears the Presbyterian Church of the charge, that she has taken upon herself to do things of a like nature, . 99–106

CHAPTER VI.

Sets forth the manner in which the officers of the Church are to exercise their power—not as individuals, but as members of assemblies or courts, the lower court being in subordination to the higher; in doing this the authority for the assembly, presbytery, and session, is produced, ... 107–117

CHAPTER VII.

On the appointment of office-bearers, refers to the fact that ecclesiastical power is vested in the whole Church as a body, and from this argues that all her members—both officers and private members—have a part to act in the investing of men with ecclesiastical power; this it also proves from Scripture, when it shows that the private members perform their part in choosing or electing, and the elders theirs in the ceremony of ordination. In the course of the argument the nature and necessity of ordination are explained, ... 118-127

CHAPTER VIII.

Takes up the great question of the Headship of Christ; disposes of the authority of the pope and civil magistrate in the Church, and shows that Christ is the Head in the widest sense,—that He is Head of the Church as composed of both office-bearers and private members; and that no one, on any pretence whatever, can come between Him and the humblest member. It explains how this is in view of a Confession of Faith and Church Courts, ... 128-173

CHAPTER IX.

Completes our task by proving that the Scriptural Form of Church Government is that which all are bound to adopt. In the course of this argument the principle, *whatever is not forbidden is permitted*, is examined, and it is found that it will only apply, in a very limited sense, to the case of an individual regulating his own conduct, and not at all in the case of the Church when making laws for the regulation of the conduct of her members; the truth here is, *whatever is not sanctioned is prohibited*: hence the Church must find a warrant for everything which she would make obligatory on her members, ... 174-191

THE SCRIPTURAL FORM

OF

CHURCH GOVERNMENT.

CHAPTER I.

THE CHURCH.

THE question as to the Lord Jesus Christ's being the sole Head of the Church, I leave for future consideration; at present I proceed to show, that He has given to us a complete system of Church Government. As a step towards this end, I shall make a few remarks upon the Church, 1st, as to what constitutes it, and, 2nd, upon errors as to what constitutes it.

WHAT CONSTITUTES THE CHURCH.

1. The Church, stripped of everything that is incidental to her as existing in this world, is made up of those human beings who are united in one body, from the fact that they are united to Christ as a common head, implying

that they have one Lord,—Christ; one faith,—faith in Him; one baptism,—baptism by the Holy Spirit. Out of this grand essential, viz., union with Christ, all her prerogatives either directly spring, or by reason of it she comes into that position in which she can lawfully assume them.

2. As composed of human beings; as existing in this world among human beings; and as set up for purposes of Christian work, she comes to have as necessary incidents:—

a. A visible form, and some members who are not members of Christ's body,

b. An organization as a society,

c. Division, in a limited sense, into different bodies.

a. Hypocrites are unavoidable.

That mystical union between Christ and the believer cannot be seen by mortal eyes. One may be thus united to Christ, and none but himself know it. But it is his duty to make it known that he may help others; he must declare to the world that he belongs to Christ, or how can he tell the world of Christ? he must let others in Christ know of his state, or how can he edify them, or be edified? hence a profession of religion is a necessary thing, or, in other words, those who are united to Christ must take a position, in the full view of mankind, which will declare what they are; in the words of Scripture, "they must let their light so shine before men, that they may see their good works, and glorify their Father who is in heaven."* Owing to the Church's taking a visible form, or in other words, when her members spring up to show to men the reality of their invisible union with Christ by profession and work, false professors spring up with them. There are many who falsely profess what others truly profess; and what the Christian does by strength derived from Christ, the false professor counterfeits. Now we must, since we have not the power to discern spirits or read the human

---

*Matt. v. 16.

heart, take men in the Church by outward appearances; and as we have seen that the outward appearance of the Christian can be counterfeited, we are, of necessity, sometimes imposed upon, and so admit members into the Church who have no part nor lot in the matter.

It may be asked, why not, when you suspect that one is not in a state of salvation, turn him out; we reply, God has not given us any authority to do so; on the contrary, He has expressly forbidden it. Suspicion is a very unsafe thing to act upon; we might, on suspicion, turn out many who were really saved, and thus, as the hasty servants were ready to do, root up the wheat while seeking to destroy the tares. Our Lord's way is best; "Let both grow together until the harvest."*

But such false members do not, in any way, go to make her the Church of Christ; they are only an impurity unavoidable from her peculiar circumstances: the great essential, as we have already said, is union with Christ. If it is asked, how do you know that all her members are not hypocrites; I answer, if there were no true coin there would be no counterfeits; a counterfeit always supposes something valuable which is counterfeited, and as soon as the valuable ceases to exist, the counterfeit must cease; so, as soon as there are no true Church members, there will, of necessity, be no Church of Christ. There may still remain a visible body, but it will be a body of death, or, to keep up our figure, a mass of worthless metal.

b. *Organization as a society is necessary.*

The Church is composed of individuals, and at the same time, she has ends to gain common to all her members; now, wherever individuals would work for a common end, they must work under a constitution and laws, and these imply organization.

(c) *Division, in a limited sense, into different bodies, is an unavoidable incident of the Church in her present circumstances.*

---

*Matt. xiii. 30.

Why do we say *division in a limited sense*? because this division does not interfere with the great and essential principles of union. An army, for example, is one body united, it may be, under one general for a given object; and though thus united, it may still be divided into brigades, regiments, and companies. This is division in precisely the same sense that we now speak of. The Church united to Christ is one great army, but she is unavoidably divided into brigades, regiments, and companies: *e.g.*, it is a large body composed of many thousands, but it must meet in companies small enough to occupy a single building; it exists in different countries, speaking different languages, and, as it has none in common, here is necessity for another division: but still it is all the same Church, though it may be in France, Germany, England, or Scotland, or any other country; it is still the Church in France, or Germany, or England, or Scotland, or in any country where its members may happen to be.

But there is another division in the same limited sense, which we would speak of more particularly, viz., division into different denominations. Such division is, in the present state of the Church, unavoidable, and, at the same time, we humbly think, not to be deplored. We deplore the fact that there are denominational jealousies and denominational bitterness; but not that there are different denominations. We long for the time when "Ephraim shall not envy Judah, and Judah shall not vex Ephraim;"* but it is the envy and vexation which we should like to see depart, and of course all such differences as lead to envy and vexation; but we would not care to see Judah become Ephraim, nor Ephraim Judah; we need both, and we want both, each having his own peculiar physiognomy and excellencies of mind along with a generous and brotherly rivalry, which shall only tend to provoke to love and to good works.

---

*Is. xi. 13.

How does it come then that we have, in the Church, different denominations? Wherever there are different attainments in knowledge there must be difference of opinion. If my neighour's eyes are twice as powerful as mine, he can doubtless see more clearly, and the landscape will reveal many objects to him, unseen by me; and while this is the case, he must have a somewhat different notion of it from that which I have; so in the Scriptures, he who sees most clearly must differ from him who sees but very imperfectly. Again, if my neighbour have eyes no better naturally than mine, yet if he have a clear light, while I must look through the mists and partial light of dawn, many objects, clearly seen by him, will appear distorted to me; so in Scripture truth, my neighbour, from the advantages of his position, may understand more fully than I, who am in the partial darkness of early prejudices, the oracles of God. But is my neighbour justified in saying to me, even though you do understand the great truths of Scripture, yet because you cannot see all other doctrines in the same light in which I do, I will not recognise you as a Christian at all; you must not presume to preach in my pulpit, nor will I allow you to sit at the Table of the Lord with me? We think not; rather would we say, we thank God for the light you already have, and, acknowledging you as a Christian brother, we hope you will do all you can to teach, as far as you know it, the gospel to others. We cannot agree in all points with you, but you will doubtless find some who do, and as it is necessary that men should associate together for the propagation of Christianity, unite with those who hold the same doctrines as yourself, and go, preach the gospel. If you call yourselves Methodists, then we will say, God speed you, Methodists, in preaching the gospel, and in saving sinners; or, if you call yourselves Baptists, Congregationalists, Episcopalians, or by any other denominational name, still we will say the same thing, *i.e.*, as before explained, if you belong to the one great assembly distinguished from the world by faith in

Christ as the Saviour of sinners. But we cannot agree with you as to all things of minor importance, and so we will associate ourselves together as Presbyterians, and go to the great work of preaching the gospel, bound to the same Lord as yourselves, under the same Head, a part of the same great Church of Christ of which you form a part. Thus we have denominational differences and a real unity, entirely different from the nominal unity of the Romish and English Churches, which are indeed rent into factions.

It may here be asked, do you think denominational differences of no importance whatever. We do not think so at all, and we now go on to show in what sense we think that

Denominational differences are important.

Though we hold what we have written above, yet we do not think, as some profess to do, that it is no matter to what denomination a man belongs. It is the whole Church composed of different denominations that is "the light of the world;" but, by means of different denominations, she sets this light up in different places, and with different degrees of brightness. As all this light is but a reflected light, Christ Himself being the true light, it follows that it will be bright or dim, just in proportion as it is the light from Christ or otherwise; or to drop figures, denominations will be safe guides, just in proportion as they are teachers of the whole truth, or teachers of some truth, or some truth mixed with error; therefore it is of the greatest importance that I, desirous of doing my part in enlightening the world, should connect myself to that society which holds up the brightest light, or teaches the way of God most perfectly. Nor is it the good of others alone that is concerned. I myself, as a Christian, live and grow spiritually by feeding on the truth, and though it may be said that one, who has the Bible, has the truth, still it is hard for a man to get different views of truth from those taught by the denomination with which he has connected himself; and it is therefore of the greatest importance, for my own sake, that I should lay aside denominational and other prejudices and come again and again to the truth, to ascertain whether I belong to the most enlightened denomination.

We may perhaps make this subject clearer by an illustration. The author of OUR CHURCH AND HER SERVICES says, page 37, "Salvation is in Christ; out of Him we are unsaved." This is the truth, and all who remember it, and act upon it, will be saved. But on page 34 he makes use of the following illustration, "Suppose we were called upon to make a perilous descent down one of the cliffs of Dover, and our *chance of safety* consisted in attaching a rope to some post at the top, would it not be of immense importance to select a strong rope and a sound post? No effort of our own would make us secure, if the support on which we depended proved worthless." The conclusion is that we should attach ourselves to a sound Church, *i.e.*, to a sound denomination, viz., the Church of England. Again on page 35 of the same work, the Church of England is compared to a ship, and the conclusion is, "She is a vessel of safety in which we may embark with perfect confidence on the voyage of life. She has borne others safely to the haven where they would be; and safely too will she bear us, if we are faithful to her, and trust to her guidance." In another place* we have these words, "Oh how much have those to answer for, who rend and divide the body of Christ's people! A branch cannot be torn away from its parent stem without suffering from it. And it is a fearful thing to cut one's self off from our Mother Church" (the Church of England as is shown by the context). All this, we do not hesitate to say, is false, and every one who believes it, and acts upon it, must undoubtedly be lost. In descending the cliff, it is plain, everything de-

---

* P. 31.

pends upon the rope and the post, and if either give way, the luckless one descending must perish, but if the Church of England ceased to exist to-morrow, every one of her members in Christ would be just as safe as ever. In crossing the ocean everything depends on the ship's keeping afloat, if she sink every passenger must be lost, but if the Church of England were swept away this moment, every one of her members united to Christ would be as safe, if not safer than ever. Again, in separating one's self from the Church of England, there is not necessarily a rent made in the body of Christ, inasmuch as the tie which binds one to a denomination, is not the tie which binds one to Christ. I do not now stop to speak of the confusion of thought found in the same book, where the rope is first made to represent Christ, p. 34, and next faith in Christ, p. 35, at the bottom, while the author intends by it the Church of England; where the ship is said to have taken others to heaven, and it is promised that she will also take us safely too, if we trust ourselves to her, and again that we may be in her "and yet be found unsaved at last."* How is this, does the ship land her passengers at two places, or does it sometimes happen that an unskilful crew gets hold of her, and a whole ship-load goes to destruction? Then we would say do not embark in that ship. But we must remember that we introduced the above as an illustration. We give it as an example of the teaching of a particular denomination, and we feel justified in doing so, for it is, in point of fact, a very good example of the kind of teaching to be found in the BOOK OF COMMON PRAYER; it is put forth by a Metropolitan, who surely ought to know the doctrines of a Church which he recommends so highly: now our conclusion is, that it is of great importance whether we belong to this denomination or not; if another can be found which teaches such truths as it teaches, without its pernicious errors, we say that it

---

* P. 37.

should be left at once, and, so far from any sin being committed, the person leaving it will render service to the cause of truth by letting his light shine where it will not be rendered useless by the will-o'-the-wisps of false doctrines set up around it.

Again, though it is becoming for Christians to regard with charity and brotherly love those denominations which differ from them on things of minor importance, *i.e.*, of minor importance compared with the great and essential doctrines of salvation, we still hold that error in such things is of great moment; for these little errors, like the small breaks in the dyke, which when left unrepaired go on increasing until the whole is swept away, and the country flooded, ever grow greater and greater until the essential doctrines themselves are undermined and overthrown. It was but small errors which at the first crept into the Christian Church, but, in the course of time, they turned it into that great apostasy the Roman Catholic Church. The Church of England was once truly Protestant, but she foolishly retained some of the apparently unimportant forms and doctrines of Rome, and the consequence is now, that the whole High-Church party has abandoned the principles of the Reformation, and the perverts from it to Romanism may be counted by hundreds. But how is the evil to be avoided? certainly not by making of all denominations one outwardly united Church. We have already seen that such a Church may have within it greater differences of opinion than exist between separate denominations, and the very fact that all these different parties are united in one denomination, prevents them, in a great measure, from watching and helping each other. Here then is one of the advantages of different denominations in the Church, they can watch and help each other, and here too is the

Good to be gained by discussing denominational differences.

It is possible that no one denomination is yet in possession of the whole truth; it is possible that each has some error: by bringing our own principles and those of other people again and again to the only true test, we may correct error, and gain higher views of truth, and thus advance nearer and nearer the point when we shall all hold the truth and see eye to eye. In one point my neighbour may be right and I may be wrong; it is his duty to show me by the Word of God where I am wrong, and what he thinks is right: again I may be right and he may be wrong; it is then my duty to show him his error, and also the truth as I see it. In this way we get all the advantages of each other's teaching: now all this is done in the discussion of denominational differences. That Church then, united by faith in Christ and baptism by the Holy Spirit, comprising within it all denominations which have this faith and baptism, is a far more truly united Church, and is a Church far better fitted to teach the truth to the world than any such humanly united Church as that of Rome.

ERRORS AS TO WHAT CONSTITUTES THE CHURCH.

1. That of the Romanist.

The Papist contends that there can be no Church without communion with one visible head, the Pope, the supposed successor of a supposed chief of the Apostles, viz., Peter; and that all in communion with the same can be admitted by him to heaven, while all others can be, and are, excluded, and given over to everlasting damnation by virtue of the same power.

In another place we shall show that such claims are not only preposterous but blasphemous.

2. That of the English High Churchman.

He holds that the prerogatives of the Church arise from the fact that they have been transmitted through an unbroken succession of regularly ordained bishops extending from the time of the Apostles to the present; and that none can exercise authority in the Church, or have any right to preach the gospel, unless ordained by one of such an unbroken succession. Thus the Churchman acknowledges the Papist and the members of the Greek Church to be members of the Christian Church, while both Papist and Greek agree in cutting him off.

In reference to this error, we have to say here, that there is no apparent ground for it at all, except the pride of the human heart, for

a. Apostolical succession is a mere figment, unsupported by either Scripture or history.

b. Even though it were a fact and not a figment, there is not a word in Scripture to show that it would convey any privilege whatever.

c. There is much in both Scripture and history to show that it is not of light but of darkness.

We do not care to burden our pages with long quotations; we make one exception, however, in order to give the judgment of a writer who, while he was the very opposite of one possessed of strong denominational prejudices, was a most thorough historian, and in every way capable of giving a just judgment as to the value of apostolical succession. Says Macaulay in his review of GLADSTONE ON CHURCH AND STATE, "What evidence, then, have we for the fact of the apostolical succession? And here we may easily defend the truth against Oxford with the same arguments with which, in old times, the truth was defended by Oxford against Rome. In this stage of our combat with Mr. Gladstone, we need few weapons except those which we find in the well-furnished and well-ordered armoury of Chillingworth.

The transmission of orders from the apostles to an English clergyman of the present day must have been through a very great number of intermediate persons. Now it is probable that no clergyman in the Church of England can trace up his spiritual genealogy from bishop to bishop, even so far back as the time of the Reformation. There remains fifteen or sixteen hundred years during which the history of the transmission of his orders is buried in utter darkness. And whether he be a priest, by succession from the apostles, depends on the question, whether, during that long period, some thousands of events took place, any one of which may, without any gross improbability, be supposed not to have taken place, We have not a tittle of evidence to any one of these events. We do not even know the names or countries of the men to whom it was taken for granted that these events happened. We do not even know whether the spiritual ancestors of any one of our contemporaries were Spanish or Arminian, Arian or Orthodox. In the utter absence of all particular evidence, we are surely entitled to require that there should be very strong evidence indeed, that the strictest regularity was observed in every generation; and that episcopal functions were exercised by none who were not bishops by succession from the apostles. But we have no such evidence. In the first place, we have not full and accurate information touching the polity of the Church during the century that followed the persecution of Nero. That, during this period, the overseers of all the little Christian societies scattered through the Roman Empire held their spiritual authority by virtue of holy orders derived from the apostles, cannot be proved by contemporary testimony, or by any testimony which can be regarded as decisive. The question, whether the primitive ecclesiastical constitution bore a greater resemblance to the Anglican or to the Calvinistic model has been fiercely disputed. It is a question on which men of eminent parts, learning, and piety have differed, and to this day differ very widely. It is a question on which, at least a full half of the ability and erudition of Protestant Europe has, ever since the Reformation, been opposed to the Anglican pretensions. Mr. Gladstone himself, we are persuaded, would have the candour to allow that, if no evidence were admitted but that which is furnished by the genuine Christian literature of the first two centuries, judgment would not go in favour of prelacy. And if he looked at the subject as calmly as he would look at the controversy respecting the Roman Comitia or the Anglo-Saxon Witenagemote, he would probably think that the absence of contemporary evidence during so long a period was a defect which later attestations, however numerous, could but very imperfectly supply.

It is surely impolitic to rest the doctrines of the English Church on an historical theory, which, to ninety-nine Protestants out of a hundred, would seem much more questionable than any of those doctrines. Nor is this all. Extreme obscurity overhangs the history of the middle ages; and the facts which are discernible through that obscurity prove that the Church was extremely ill regulated. We read of sees of the highest dignity openly sold, transferred backwards and forwards by popular tumult—bestowed sometimes by a profligate woman on her paramour—sometimes by a warlike baron on a kinsman, still a stripling. We read of bishops of ten years old—of bishops of five years old—of many popes who were mere boys, and who rivalled the frantic dissoluteness of Caligula—nay, of a female pope. And though this last story, once believed throughout all Europe, has been disproved by the strict researches of modern criticism, the most discerning of those who reject it have admitted that it is not intrinsically improbable. In our own island, it was the complaint of Alfred that not a single priest, south of the Thames, and very few on the north, could read either Latin or English. And this illiterate clergy exercised their ministry amidst a rude and half heathen population, in which Danish pirates, unchristened, or christened by the hundred on a field of battle, were mingled with the Saxon peasantry scarcely better instructed in religion. The state of Ireland was still worse. '*Tota illa per universam Hiberniam dissolutio ecclesiasticæ disciplinæ,—illa ubique pro consuetudine Christiana sæva subintroducta barbaries*'*—are the ex-

---

* That total destruction of Church discipline throughout the whole of Ireland,—that cruel barbarity everywhere introduced in the place of Christian usage.

pressions of St. Bernard. We are, therefore, at a loss to conceive how any clergyman can feel confident that his orders have come down correctly. Whether he be really a successor of the apostles depends on an immense number of such contingencies as these,—whether under King Ethelwolf, a stupid priest might not, while baptizing several scores of Danish prisoners who had just made their option between the font and the gallows, inadvertently omit to perform the rite on one of these graceless proselytes?—whether, in the seventh century, an impostor, who had never received consecration, might not have passed himself off as a bishop on a rude tribe of Scots? —whether a lad of twelve did really, by a ceremony huddled over when he was too drunk to know what he was about, convey the episcopal character to a lad of ten?

Since the first century, not less, in all probability, than a hundred thousand persons have exercised the functions of bishops. That many of these have not been bishops by apostolical succession is quite certain. Hooker admits that deviations from the general rule have been frequent, and with a boldness worthy of his high and statesmanlike intellect, pronounces them to have been often justifiable. 'There may be,' says he, 'sometimes very just and sufficient reason to allow ordination made without a bishop. Where the Church must needs have some ordained, and neither hath, nor can have possibly, a bishop to ordain, in case of such necessity the ordinary institution of God hath given *oftentimes*, and may give place. And therefore we are not simply without exception to urge a lineal descent of power from the apostles by continued succession of bishops in every effectual ordination.' There can be little doubt, we think, that the succession, if it ever existed, has often been interrupted in ways much less respectable. For example, let us suppose —and we are sure no person will think the supposition by any means improbable—that, in the third century, a man of no principle and some parts, who has, in the course of a roving and discreditable life, been a catechumen at Antioch, and has there become familiar with Christian usages and doctrines, afterwards rambles to Marseilles, where he finds a Christian society, rich, liberal, and simple-hearted. He pretends to be a Christian, attracts notice by his abilities and affected zeal, and is raised to the episcopal dignity without having ever been baptized. That such an event might happen, nay, was very likely to happen, cannot well be disputed by any one who has read the life of Peregrinus. The very virtues, indeed, which distinguished the early Christians, seem to have laid them open to those arts which deceived

> ' Uriel, though Regent of the Sun, and held
> The sharpest-sighted spirit of all in heaven.'

Now, this unbaptized impostor is evidently no successor of the apostles. He is not even a Christian; and all orders derived through such a pretended bishop are altogether invalid. Do we know enough of the state of the world and of the Church in the third century, to be able to say with confidence that there were not at that time twenty such pretended bishops? every such case makes a break in the apostolic succession.

Now, suppose that a break, such as Hooker admits to have been both common and justifiable, or such as we have supposed to be produced by hypocrisy and cupidity, were found in the chain which connected the apostles with any of the missionaries who first spread Christianity in the wilder parts of Europe—who can say how extensive the effect of this single break may be? Suppose that St. Patrick, for example, if ever there was such a man, or Theodore of Tarsus, who is said to have consecrated in the seventh century the first bishops of many English sees, had not the true apostolical orders, is it not conceivable that such a circumstance may affect the orders of many clergymen now living? Even if it were possible, which it assuredly is not, to prove that the Church had the apostolical orders in the third century, it would be impossible to prove that those orders were not in the twelfth century so far lost that no ecclesiastic could be certain of the legitimate descent of his own spiritual character: and if this were so, no subsequent precautions could repair the evil.

Chillingworth states the conclusion at which he had arrived on this subject in these very remarkable words: 'That of ten thousand probables no one should be false; that of ten thousand requisites, whereof any one may fail, not one should be wanting, this to me is extremely improbable, and even cousin-german to impossible. So that the assurance hereof is like a machine composed of an innumerable multitude of pieces, of which it is strangely unlikely but some will be out of order; and yet, if any piece be so, the whole fabric falls of necessity to the ground: and he that shall put them together, and maturely consider all the possible ways of lapsing and nullifying a priesthood in the Church of Rome, will be very inclinable to think that it is a hundred to one, that among a hundred seeming priests, there is not one true one; nay, that it is not a thing very improbable that, amongst those many millions which make up the Romish hierarchy, there are not twenty true.' We do not pretend to know to what precise extent the canonists of Oxford agree with those of Rome as to the circumstances which nullify orders. We will not, therefore, go so far as Chillingworth. We only say that we see no satisfactory proof of the fact, that the Church of England possesses the apostolical succession."

What does the reader think of apostolical succession? A wretched figment indeed is apostolical succession. What must the reader think of that denomination, or rather of those in it, who, assuming that such a figment is that without which a church cannot exist, proceed to unchurch other denominations, and sneer at them as "*sects,*" even though it is manifest, when they are tried by Scripture tests, that they are parts of that Church which is united by being united to Christ, the " one Lord"—united by a common

THE CHURCH. 27

faith in that "one Lord"—united by a common baptism by the Holy Spirit? What must be thought of the common sense and religious feeling of those who think that apostolical succession is a better bond of unity than faith in Christ? Let those who can be satisfied with such a pretension be satisfied with it; but we prefer the unity indicated by the Bible.

3. *Error of the Plymouth Brethren with respect to what constitutes the Church.*

It is not very easy to get at the meaning of the Brethren in reference to the Church, nor am I sure that they themselves know what they mean, but as correctly as I have been able to ascertain from personal intercourse with members of their body, and from reading such writings as those of Kelly, I will state their views on this subject. They contend that the prerogatives of the Church arise not from union with Christ, but from the presence of the Holy Ghost in the assembly as He was present at the day of Pentecost; there may be union with Christ without this presence of the Spirit, and consequently there may be good people who are not in the Church. The Spirit presides in the Church, and calls whom He will at the time of meeting to teach and to edify the brethren; and no man, or body of men, must presume to set apart any one to the special work of preaching. All denominations, such as Episcopalians, Methodists, Baptists, Independents, and Presbyterians, are not of the Church of God, but are in opposition to His Spirit, inasmuch as they set apart men to preside over their meetings. There are good people in these denominations, but they must become Brethren (that is Plymouth Brethren) before they can belong to the Church. In the Church there are none but true believers; no tares must be tolerated among the wheat.

By showing what constitutes the Church, we have shown that, in this matter, the Plymouth Brethren are in error. Their doctrine is just as exclusive, in as far as membership in the Church is concerned, as is that of the Papist or High Churchman: by going a great way east you can arrive at the same place as if you travel a great way west. To use another figure, though somewhat trite, the Plymouth Brethren, in avoiding the Scylla of the High Churchman, have fallen into the Charybdis of Darbyism.

In the meantime we shall content ourselves with merely showing that the Church existed before the day of Pentecost, and that the Holy Spirit is not now present in her as He was then; and therefore that her prerogatives cannot arise from the facts that He on that day first constituted her the Church, and continues with her as He was present then.

It is not true that the Spirit now dwells in the Church as He manifested Himself at the day of Pentecost. He comes now unseen by mortals and changes hearts—He comes now and takes of the things that are Christ's, and shows them to us; but He does not now come in any visible form as He did on the day of Pentecost; He does not now come to give divine inspiration to any as He did then; nor yet, does He come now to confer on any miraculous gifts such as He imparted then. But as He is present now, even so was He present before the day of Pentecost, for Jesus says to Nicodemus, "Marvel not that I said unto thee, Ye must be born again. The wind bloweth where it listeth, and thou hearest the sound thereof, but canst not tell whence it cometh and whither it goeth: so is every one that is born of the Spirit." When Nicodemus, in reply, exclaimed, "How can these things be?" Jesus answered him in a way which clearly implied that this work of the Spirit had been going on all along, and that Nicodemus should have understood it, "Art thou a master of Israel and knowest not these things."*

---

*John iii. 7—10.

We might arrive at the same conclusion in another way. " Without faith," says the Scripture, " it is impossible to please God."* Every one then, who went to heaven before Christ came, as well as afterwards, must have exercised it; but faith can only be exercised by him who has been made alive by the Spirit; the Spirit must then have baptized every one of the Old Testament saints. We are expressly told that they did exercise faith. " By faith Abel offered unto God a more excellent sacrifice than Cain."† The faith of Abel must have been faith in Christ, for it was a bloody sacrifice which he offered, and unless his faith had been fixed on what that offering represented, it could not have availed him anything, as the blood of bulls and of goats cannot take away sin. Abraham had faith, and it was faith in Christ too, for Christ Himself says, " Abraham rejoiced to see my day ; and he saw it, and was glad."‡ But why need we particular examples? as we have already said, none ever went to heaven without a change of heart by the Spirit, such as our Lord implies Nicodemus should have understood ; and if the Old Testament saints had not this change, they never went there at all. The Spirit then wrought in the hearts of men before Pentecost.

By following out this same line of argument we shall also see that it is not true that the Church did not exist before Pentecost. Men were saved before that time by faith in Christ; and that faith must have been produced by the Spirit: they had then the " One Lord, one faith, and one baptism," which make the Church.

But why need we labour in this way to prove that the Church existed before Pentecost, when we have the direct statements of Scripture to that effect. " This is he that was in the *church* in the wilderness,"§ that is in the wilderness between Egypt and Canaan. " Christ," we are told in another place, " loved the *church*, and gave himself for it."‖ For whom then did Christ give Him-

---

*Heb. xi. 6. †Heb. xi. 4. ‡John viii. 56. §Acts vii. 38. ‖Ep. v. 25.

self; for those who should be saved after the day of Pentecost, or for those saved both before and after?

We might, in addition to what we have brought forward, show how often the same word is used for *Church* in the Greek version of the Old Testament, which is employed to designate it in the New; and by taking this along with the fact that the Apostles themselves were as familiar with that version as with the original, and that they knew that many of the people to whom they wrote were much more familiar with it than with the Hebrew,—in fine it was the only Old Testament which many of them had,—it appears then that by using the same word for the New Testament Church, which was used in that version for the Old, they intended to teach that it was one and the same Church from the beginning.

If it is objected here, in reference to what we have advanced about the work of the Spirit, that Christ said, "It is expedient for you that I go away; for if I go not away the Comforter will not come unto you;"* and it is supposed that this teaches that the Spirit had not previously wrought in the hearts of men, we have just to ask, why did Christ imply that Nicodemus should have known of the new birth? We have just to refer back to all the proofs that we have given of His work in the world before this; and we may add, that the disciples themselves had shown in their conduct the fruits of the Spirit before this time. Says Christ to Peter, " Blessed art thou Simon Barjona: for flesh and blood hath not revealed it unto thee, but my Father which is in heaven."† How does the Father make known such truths to creatures—is it not by His Spirit? But the Comforter had not yet come to them with that inspiration and power which were necessary to fit them for their duties as Apostles, and it was expedient that He should. If it is still further objected, that, in His coming, He is to convince the world; I reply it is true, but yet it is through the Apostles, as inspired

---

*John xvi. 7.   †Matt. xvi. 17.

teachers, that He will convince it, for, mark you, it is said, "I will send him unto you, and when he is come," that is to you, "he will reprove, &c."

We now leave the error of the Plymouth Brethren for the present, but we shall notice it again in the proper place, along with others which spring from it. As we have now shown what constitutes the Church, we shall endeavour to show in the following chapter, that the Lord Jesus has given her a Ministry.

CHAPTER II.

THE MINISTRY.

IT may to some seem hardly necessary to inquire as to the Scriptural grounds for the office of the ministry, as all well-known denominations at once admit that this office is of divine appointment: and, indeed, the danger has hitherto been in the way of making too much of it. But in the last few years, a new denomination has sprung up, which goes to exactly the opposite extreme of the High Churchman. Nor need we wonder at this, for human nature is like a pendulum, the farther one moves it from the place of rest, the farther it will go to the opposite side when released. The famine-stricken will gorge themselves if food be given in sufficient quantity; the down-trodden will rush headlong into anarchy and wild excess, when once the galling power of the tyrant is overthrown; so when once the shackles of a corrupt and tyrannical church are thrown off, the liberated one, instead of stopping at the golden mean of Scripture, rushes headlong into ecclesiastical anarchy, by declaring against anything and everything bearing the name of ministry. All true believers, in the estimation of such, may publicly preach and administer the sacraments. If you ask, are ignorant men capable of preaching? the answer is, the gospel is so simple that any one can preach it. Do you ask further, can every one speak to edification? and you have the ready reply, no, but the exhortations of such as cannot edify must be borne as one of the crosses which Christ has laid upon His people. Imagining that there must be a great deal of such cross-bearing, you again ask, is it right to have the gospel preached in such a way, that the hearing of what should be glad tidings becomes a mere cross-bearing? and again it is answered, you mistake; though it is lawful for all to preach, yet all do not use their liberty: preaching, with rare exceptions, is left to such as are gifted by the Holy Ghost. We might answer all this now (we shall do so at another time), but first, as of more importance, we say that this system, if system it may be called, is, in as far as its peculiarities are concerned, opposed to the Word of God and common sense.

THE LORD JESUS HAS GIVEN A MINISTRY TO THE CHURCH.

1. Common sense might teach us that there should be a Ministry.

In order that any work may be well done, division of labour is necessary. This principle is recognized in every department of worldly affairs—in the factory, in the warehouse, on the farm, and in the college; and shall the children of this world be wiser in this respect also, than the children of light? Even though they may be, still we maintain that there should be division of labour in the Church of Christ, if it is to do its work with efficiency. Let there be no misunderstanding; we hold that the Church composed of office-bearers and private members is the city set on an high hill that cannot be hid; that all, both office-bearers and private members, are the persons upon whom this injunction, " Let your light so shine before men, that they may see your good works, and glorify your Father which is in heaven,"* is binding; in a word, that every one, whether in a public or private capacity in the Church, is bound to do all that he can to promote the advancement of Christ's kingdom; but, we hold, at the same time, that Christ's kingdom is best advanced when every one knows his own particular work, and does it. If God's people are to be edified by the

* Matt. v. 16.

teaching of divine things, it is necessary that some should give themselves specially to the study of the Word of God, so as to be able to be leaders and instructors in these things; if the poor are to be provided for, and the financial affairs of the congregation properly managed, it must be the special duty of some in particular to look after such things; and so with other works.

2. *Scripture clearly teaches by direct statements that there should be a Ministry.*

It is interesting to note that Paul, before stating plainly that Christ has given a ministry to the Church, conducts the mind to the fact by an illustration founded upon the necessity for division of labour in a particular case. "For as the body is one, and hath many members, and all the members of that one body, being many, are one body: so also is Christ. For by one Spirit are we all baptized into one body, whether we be Jews or Gentiles, whether we be bond or free; and have been all made to drink into one Spirit. For the body is not one member but many. If the foot shall say, because I am not the hand I am not of the body; is it therefore not of the body? and if the ear shall say; Because I am not the eye, I am not of the body; is it therefore not of the body? If the whole body were an eye, where were the hearing? if the whole were hearing, where were the smelling?" The intended application of this is manifestly as follows:—The Church, though one body, inasmuch as it has all been baptized by one Spirit, is not all made up of preachers, but has members engaged in various duties. If the private member shall say, because I am not a preacher I have no duties to perform, has he therefore no duties to perform? and if the deacon shall say, because I am not the elder, I am not under obligation to do anything, is he therefore not under obligation to do anything? If all were preachers, where were the people to preach to; if all were rulers, where were the ruled; if all are to be obeyed, where were those whose duty it is to obey? Paul proceeds, " But now hath God set the members every one of them in the body, as it hath pleased him. And if they were all one member, where were the body? But now are they many members, yet but one body. And the eye cannot say unto the hand, I have no need of thee; nor again the head to the feet, I have no need of you. Nay, much more those members of the body which seem to be more feeble, are necessary: And those members of the body, which we think to be less honourable, upon these we bestow more abundant honour; and our uncomely parts have more abundant comeliness. For our comely parts have no need; but God hath tempered the body together, having given more abundant honour to that part which lacked: that there should be no schism in the body; but that the members should have the same care one for another. And whether one member suffer, all the members suffer with it; or one member be honoured, all the members rejoice with it." By the above he teaches, that God has given to the members of the Church such offices as it has pleased Him, for if all had the same office, how would the Church be a perfect organization? The private member cannot say to the officer, I have no need of thee; nor yet the one officer to another, I have no need of thee: there should be no jealousy, but each member of the Church, no matter what his position, should care for his fellow-member, as his fellow-member should care for him, so that there may be no schism in the body. We would here invite those who are so fond of the word *schism* to observe its meaning; he is the schismatic who rebels against the organization of the Church as laid down in Scripture, and refuses to be anything unless he can be everything; who cries out, we have no need of a Ministry, all believers are preachers, or any believer may preach.

Paul follows up his pointed illustration by this emphatic statement, " Now ye are the body of Christ and members in particular. And *God hath set some in the Church,* first apostles, secondly prophets, thirdly teachers, after that miracles, then gifts of healing, helps, governments, diversities of tongues. Are all apostles? are all prophets? are all teachers? are all workers of miracles? Have all the gift of healing? do all speak with tongues? do all interpret?"* It may be asked here, what right have you to explain this passage in reference to any church organization now in existence; how can you show that it gives you authority to have ministers, and not apostles, prophets, and others who, you say, no longer exist? We do not answer this question now, because we shall consider it a few pages farther on.

3. The provision made for those who preach the Gospel shows that this work is assigned to a special class.

Those who preach the Gospel are to be supported by those who hear it. Says Paul, "Do ye not know that they which minister about holy things, live of the things of the temple? and they which wait at the altar, are partakers with the altar? Even so hath the Lord ordained that they which preach the Gospel should live of the Gospel."† What becomes of the theory that there is to be no paid Ministry, indeed, no Ministry at all?

4. It is proved that there is a Ministry by the fact, that private members are called upon to obey their rulers in the Church.

In the Epistle to the Hebrews it is said, "Obey them that have the rule over you, and submit yourselves."‡ The ministers are the rulers here spoken of, because it is added "They watch for your souls:" this is the minister's duty. In the same chapter where it is enjoined, "Remember them which have the rule over you," it is added, "Who have spoken unto you the word of God." Ministers are elders and elders are rulers. "Let the elders that

---

* I Cor. xii. † I Cor. ix. 13, 14. ‡ Heb. xiii. 17.

rule well be counted worthy of double honour, especially they who labour in the word and doctrine."* It is plain then that there must be two classes in the Church, a governing and a governed, and also that ministers belong to the governing class, and must therefore be distinct from the other members of the Church. What then becomes of the theory, that all believers in the Church are on precisely the same footing, in a word, that all are at once preachers and private members.

5. It is proved that a Ministry should still exist by the fact that the need for it still exists.

"When He ascended up on high, He led captivity captive and gave gifts unto men. * * * And he gave some apostles; and some prophets; and some evangelists; and some pastors and teachers; *for the perfecting of the saints, for the work of the ministry, for the edifying of the body of Christ.*"† Is not the *work* of the Ministry needed now as well as in the days of the Apostles? Does the body of Christ not need edification now as much as it ever did? do not the saints of to-day need perfecting as much as those of primitive times? Our opponents must answer all these questions in the affirmative. Why then, we ask, are we not to have a Ministry for the accomplishment of such desirable ends? If the Apostles, inspired by God, judged a Ministry the best thing to do this work, it is surely not for us to question their arrangement. If it is asked, why do you not have all the offices here spoken of; if you argue for a Ministry from this passage, why not have the same kind of a Ministry which it sets forth? We answer, we have precisely the kind of Ministry it sets forth. But says one, you have no apostles; for a good reason, we reply. The work of apostles, prophets, and other extraordinary officers, may be done once and for all, and forever remains for edification after they have passed

---

* 1 Tim. v. 17. † Eph. iv. 8, 11, 12.

away; but that of the pastor and teacher can only remain by pastors and teachers themselves remaining; hence we conclude, that while out of the early Ministry, apostles, prophets, and some others have gone, that pastors, teachers, helps, and governments, still remain; and these are all that we can say the passage, fairly interpreted according to the light given to us, sets forth as Church officers.

6. *The qualifications necessary for the office of the Ministry are pointed out, and this shows that it is the intention of the Head of the Church that there should be a Ministry.*

Titus was to ordain elders in every city, and the qualifications for that office are specified as follows, "If any be blameless, the husband of one wife, having faithful children, not accused of riot or unruly. For a bishop must be blameless, as the steward of God; not self-willed, not soon angry, not given to wine, no striker, not given to filthy lucre; but a lover of hospitality, a lover of good men, sober, just, holy, temperate; holding fast the faithful word as he hath been taught, that he may be able by sound doctrine both to exhort and to convince the gainsayers."* If, as some say, there should be no Ministry at all, and as others say that man has not in any way the appointment of the minister to his office, what use is there in telling us of the qualifications for the office, which are to guide us in our selection.

7. *It is proved that there should be a Ministry by the fact that the private members are called upon to elect men to the office of the Ministry.*

Even when the deacons, subordinate officers in the Church, were needed, the whole body of the disciples were called upon to look out men of such and such quali-

---

* Titus, i. 6—9.

fications, that they might be ordained by the Apostles, and that elders or ministers were also chosen in this manner is shown by these words, "When they had ordained them elders in every church,"* which in the original clearly means *when they had elders elected for them by show of hands.*

8. *The Apostles have given us a particular form by which to invest men with the ministerial office.*

Says Paul to Timothy, "Neglect not the gift that is in thee, which was given thee by prophecy, with the laying on of the hands of the presbytery."† The laying on of the hands of the presbytery here evidently refers to the formal setting apart of Timothy to the office of the Ministry, for we find in the case of the deacons, the same form used in setting them apart to their office, and also in the setting apart of Paul and Barnabas to a special mission. How is it that we have this form, if there is no special office such as that of the Ministry in the Church?

We may be told here that we do not do our opponents justice; but we can truly say that we are anxious to do them justice. We think that our Ministry is appointed by authority of the Word of God, and they have used language concerning it, which justifies us in concluding that they deny that the Scripture authorizes us to have a Ministry. Let us however take the views of the most advanced of the Brethren, those who have learned something from other denominations, and see what they amount to. To those who deny altogether the divine authority for the appointment of the Ministry, we have already given some of the scriptural grounds for that appointment. We might have given more, but we have thought it unnecessary to multiply proofs of a doctrine so clearly taught. We shall now take up the notions of the more advanced of our opponents in reference to this subject.

---

* Acts, xiv. 23.   † 1 Tim. iv. 14.

We shall take Mr. Kelly as the exponent of their views. With respect to his statement that "there was no such thing as the Church till the death of Christ," we simply remark, that it is not only an assertion without anything to back it, but as we have already seen, an assertion in the face of most weighty evidence to the contrary. He thus proceeds *in his way* to show, that on the day of Pentecost the Holy Ghost first baptized God's people into what he calls "*the assembly*," and what we call the *Church*. Since that time, the Holy Spirit has been present in the assembly dividing His gifts to every man severally as He will. "Ministry," then, "may be defined to be the exercise of gift," and again, "the Holy Spirit is present in the assembly to edify it by whomsoever He will."*

Since the very commencement of the Christian dispensation, and we suppose, long before it, there have been those who have mistaken their proper place in the world and the Church. There were those who would follow Christ when it would be better for them and the world that they should be at home; there have been many who have sought and obtained high places, and were unable when they got them to fill them; and there have been many who imagined that they had a special call to enlighten their brethren in the way of preaching, while it has been very plain, at least to many of the brethren, that there were no qualifications at all possessed by such zealous individuals, who would thrust themselves forward as preachers, and that the good work was rather retarded than forwarded by their doing so. And just as we have always had such preachers, we have had along with them a class of persons who think it wrong to put any check upon what appears to them a laudable desire to advance the cause of Christ, even though such teachers in their attempts only succeed in edifying themselves and distracting every one else. It is for the special benefit of this mute and inglorious class—mute and inglorious

---

* Lectures on the Church of God, *passim*.

through what have been sneered at as *"men's rules"*—that the theory of Kelly and others of his school has been invented. We say *invented*, because if Mr. Kelly will calmly consider, he will perceive that the baptism of the Spirit did not make the Ministry, as all the Ministry which was at that time necessary had been before appointed; it only fitted that Ministry for its special work, viz., the setting up of the order of things to be followed in the Christian Church, along with the completion of the canon of Scripture. Further, he will perceive that the Holy Spirit, though now present in the Church to " take of the things that are Christ's and shew them to us," is not present to give men divine inspiration, nor yet to impart miraculous gifts.

But still the zealous convert who wishes to " speak," professes to be under the guidance of the Spirit, and most certainly those who put themselves in his way resist the Spirit. The taking up of such a notion as the above has been the germ from which such labours as those of Mr. Kelly—to prove that the Spirit is always present in the assembly to edify by whom He will, that is, to edify by whoever takes it into his head that he is gifted,—have sprung. Oh, no, say the Plymouth Brethren, the brethren judge as to who is gifted or not. Admit then that the Spirit now confers no miraculous gift, and Mr. Kelly admits it; admit also that the brethren are the judges as to who is gifted, and it must be admitted; and we say at once, without fear of contradiction, that it is quite possible to have a Ministry in perfect harmony with these principles; and that the Presbyterian Church, for example, and it is not the only one, is in these things as little opposed to the Spirit as are the Plymouth Brethren; while in other respects, it carries out His directions where they refuse to do so; it has, in accordance with His word, a special Ministry, whereas they will not have any. We now proceed to show that the Presbyterian Church acts in accordance with principles which the Plymouth Brethren must admit to be true.

In order to arrive at a clear understanding of this subject, let us inquire

1. What are the gifts now enjoyed by the Church of God?

They are :—

a. Physical gifts, such as sufficient strength of body, proper formation of the vocal organs, hearing, seeing, &c.

b. Intellectual gifts, such as command of language, the power of studying, and of imparting knowledge to others.

c. Moral gifts, such as the power of mind, which enables one to judge between right and wrong, and also the force of character which enables him to choose the right and leave the wrong, and so to live an upright and moral life.

These three kinds of gifts are possessed by many of the men of the world, as well as by many Christians, though some of them are strengthened when one becomes a Christian.

d. Spiritual gifts, including all that is summed up in Regeneration or the new heart.

These last are possessed by all Christians in common, but not by men of the world.

e. Over and above all the gifts just mentioned, he who aspires to the office of the Ministry should have a firm conviction that it is his duty to preach, so firm a conviction that he is compelled to exclaim, " Woe is unto me, if I preach not the gospel."* This conviction arises from the love of Christ " shed abroad in the heart," and the consequent love of the sinner, along with a consideration of his own gifts and his duty, as set forth in the Word ; the Spirit in all this helping him as He helps any of God's children when they seek spiritual truths.

There are no gifts now enjoyed by any, different in kind from those which we have pointed out ; if any one

---

*I Cor. ix. 16.

should claim more, we have a right to demand, as a proof of such claim, direct evidence from God, and failing this, we should have no hesitation in pronouncing him an impostor.

2. *How does the Presbyterian Church act in reference to the gifted?*

a. No man, professing to be gifted, is turned away by her without a fair trial.

b. No man, *properly gifted*, is kept back by her from the office of the Ministry.

c. The trial of gifts is made by the whole of God's people, *i.e.*, by both private members and office-bearers.

We can show the above propositions to be strictly true.

We have no desire in the Presbyterian Church to keep men from preaching the Gospel, on the contrary, " we pray the Lord of the harvest to send forth labourers into his harvest." But when any one comes forth and declares, " I believe that I am called to preach the Gospel," do we at once give him official standing as a minister? certainly not. It is the duty of every body of Christians to try such first, and the Lord Himself commends the Church for so doing.* The candidate is then examined as to his grounds for believing that he is called to preach. 1. As to his spiritual gifts; 2, as to his intellectual and moral gifts: if he gives perfect satisfaction in all these matters, the Presbytery then says to him, as far as we are able to judge, we think you are called to preach the gospel, but there is another test which you must undergo; it is not in our power to give you official standing as a minister until you are tried and accepted by God's people as one who has gifts for edification; so we give you authority to preach before them, and as soon as a company of them shall signify to us that you are an acceptable preacher, we will come and set you apart, in the Scrip-

---

*See Rev. ii. 2.

tural way, to the office of the Ministry by the laying on of hands.

If the candidate cannot satisfy the Presbytery that he has the spiritual and moral qualifications, he is, at least for the time, rejected; but it generally happens that he has not the proper intellectual qualifications; even though he may have intellectual strength, he may not have intellectual cultivation, and under such circumstances, he is certified to a college where he may be trained. During this course of training his conduct is noted, and he is again and again examined as to all his gifts until the close of his course, when a special examination on the same takes place, and if it proves satisfactory, he is sent forth, as in the former case, for his trial before the private members of the Church, after which, if he is accepted by a congregation, he is ordained to the office of the Ministry.

Wherein is Brethrenism superior to the above? "Oh!" says one, "we allow the Holy Ghost to edify the assembly by whomsoever He pleases." So do we, I answer. "But you undertake to say a man is qualified or not, and, until you think he is qualified, he must not preach." He may preach if he can get any one to listen to him, but we do not give him the standing of a minister until we think him qualified. And how, may I ask, do you do with those who want to speak in your assembly, if they are not gifted? "The assembly judges as to gifts, and only allows those to speak who can edify." That is precisely what we do; our assembly composed of both ministers and people judges of gifts, as I have shown, and only accepts those who can speak to edification.

Thus we have all the advantages which the Plymouth Brethren can claim for their system, without any of the disadvantages of theirs. Besides, we have many positive advantages over them. We make a much more satisfactory trial of gifts than they do. We give men a time of probation before we accept them as ministers; and if the Brethren and some other denominations would follow our example, they would not be so often imposed upon by canting hypocrites as at present. During this term of probation, in the case of all not intellectually qualified, we require a thorough course of training in those subjects most useful to him who would rightly divide the word of truth. If asked here, what necessity there is for human learning, we would just refer our interrogator to a consideration of the gifts now possessed by men; while every man of ordinary common sense knows well what need there is, without my taking the trouble to show, as I easily could do, were this the place for it, most pressing need. Further, we obey the Holy Spirit in selecting men, and in setting them apart to the office of the Ministry, *i.e.*, we follow the directions which He has given on this matter; while the Brethren do not. We would just add one word of warning to those who are so forward to pronounce us usurpers of the place of the Holy Ghost in the Church, to beware lest they are found despisers of Christ, for He said, "He that despiseth you despiseth Me; and he that despiseth Me despiseth him that sent Me."*

---

* Luke x. 16.

CHAPTER III.

OF WHAT OFFICERS DOES THE MINISTRY CONSIST?

WE are told by Paul that "God hath set some in the Church, first apostles, secondarily prophets, thirdly teachers, after that miracles, then gifts of healings, helps, governments, diversities of tongues;"* and again, "He gave some, apostles; and some, prophets; and some, evangelists; and some, pastors and teachers."† If all things had continued as they were at the commencement of the Christian dispensation, we should now have just the above-mentioned officers in the Christian Ministry, neither more nor less. But things have not remained as they were, for

SOME OF THE OFFICERS GIVEN BY CHRIST TO HIS CHURCH WERE EXTRAORDINARY, AND HAVE CEASED; OTHERS ARE ORDINARY AND PERPETUAL.

In the commencement of every dispensation of divine appointment, we may naturally and reasonably look for two things, first, a set of officers to introduce the new order of things, and secondly, another set to continue the order of things thus established. The former must be directly taught of God, *i. e.*, they must either be taught

---

* 1 Cor. xii, 28.   † Eph. iv, 11.

OF WHAT OFFICERS DOES THE MINISTRY CONSIST? 47

by His speaking to them, or by the inspiration of the Holy Ghost, what God will have done, and they must also have a commission immediately from Him to do it. A moment's reflection will show, that what is done by men so qualified, is done by God, and is therefore perfect, and that it remains for our guidance until He shall inform us by another revelation that He has something new for us. Nor is it with these men as with mere human legislators, whose works are imperfect; the latter need successors to alter and amend as the necessities of the case may require; the former, being instructed by One who knew all the necessities which had arisen, or ever would arise, established a perfect order of things, and made perfect laws, and therefore have no need of successors. The second set of officers mentioned need not be inspired or directly commissioned by God, by reason of the teaching of the first, and of the system of government which they have established; and as it belongs to the former to continue a certain order of things as long as the world stands (for we have no right to expect another revelation), they must of necessity have successors; hence we conclude that *some of the officers given by Christ to His Church were extraordinary and have ceased; that others are ordinary and perpetual.*

APOSTLES, PROPHETS, EVANGELISTS, WORKERS OF MIRACLES, THOSE POSSESSING GIFTS OF HEALING, AND THOSE HAVING THE POWER TO SPEAK MIRACULOUSLY IN DIFFERENT LANGUAGES, HAVE CEASED; THE REST REMAIN.

We have next, in the investigation of this subject, to ascertain what officers have passed away, and we shall then know what ones remain. We do not now undertake anything either doubtful or difficult of accomplishment, as we have sure and safe landmarks to guide us. We may lay it down at the outset as certain, that no church officer can now lay claim to inspiration, the power of working miracles, or a commission directly from God authorizing him to do a particular work; hence, if we can find that one or all these things were the necessary qualifications of any of those officers mentioned as given to the Church, we know most certainly that such officer has ceased. Again, we know what works were required, while the Church was being established in the new order of things, which are not required now; hence, if we can find that it was the special duty of any of the above-mentioned officers to do these works, we may be certain that such officer has ceased, as he is now no longer needed; doubly sure then may we be, where we can apply both of these tests.

In view of both of the above tests, we can say that the Apostles, as such, were extraordinary officers. It was necessary, in the first place, that the Apostles should be

1. Inspired.

That *it was necessary that they should be inspired is proved* by their being commanded to wait in Jerusalem until the promise of the Father should be sent upon them,* which promise was the inspiration of the Holy Ghost, as the result proved; and also by Paul's answer to the Judaizing teachers in Galatia, who had taught that he was not an Apostle. "But I certify you, brethren, that the gospel which was preached of me is not after man. For I neither received it of man, neither was I taught it, but by the revelation of Jesus Christ."† That *they were inspired* is also proved by what took place at the day of Pentecost; when "There appeared unto them cloven tongues like as of fire, and it sat upon each of them, and they were all filled with the Holy Ghost, and began to speak with other tongues, as the Spirit gave them utterance;"‡ and by the claims which they put forth in their writings, and by those writings being accepted by the Church as canonical.

---

* Luke xxiv, 49.   † Gal. i, 11, 12.   ‡ Acts ii, 3, 4.

OF WHAT OFFICERS DOES THE MINISTRY CONSIST? 49

2. Gifted with the power of working miracles.

That this was also a necessary qualification of an Apostle, Paul intimates when he says to the Corinthians, "Truly the signs of an apostle were wrought among you in all patience, in signs and wonders, and mighty deeds."* None can deny that the other Apostles also *possessed* the power of working miracles,—as there are passages of Scripture, too numerous to quote, proving the fact,— "Many wonders and signs were done by the apostles,"†

3. Personal acquaintances of the Lord Jesus.

They all had this qualification, and it was *necessary*. Peter supposed so when he said, "Of these men which have companied with us all the time that the Lord Jesus went in and out among us, beginning from the baptism of John, unto that same day that he was taken up from us, must one be ordained to be a witness with us of his resurrection."‡ Paul likewise teaches the same thing, saying, "Am I not an apostle? * * * have I not seen Jesus Christ our Lord?"§

4. Commissioned by Christ Himself.

The Apostles all held their commissions directly from Christ, and could not have been properly and lawfully constituted Apostles without such direct commission. The nature of their work proves this; it was about things hitherto unrevealed, and, as a matter of course, they needed authority from the great Head.

If it be objected here that Matthias did not hold his commission directly from Christ, I reply, it is true, but nevertheless, this case is in our favour rather than against us; for whatever view we may take of his apostleship or supposed apostleship, it appears from the following consideration that the disciples thought that a direct appoint-

---

* 2 Cor. xii, 12. † Acts ii, 43. ‡ Acts i, 21, 22. § 1 Cor. ix, 1.

ment from God was necessary: they did not presume to say which of the two men chosen should be the apostle, but they prayed to God, saying, "Thou, Lord, which knowest the hearts of all men, show whether of these two *thou* hast chosen."* It is possible, and, I think, probable, as I shall presently show, that the disciples were here mistaken, but yet they supposed that they were getting an appointment directly from God. If God recognized this appointment, it was one directly from Him;† if He did not, all is conceded which we ask.

We think however, that Matthias was never owned by the Lord as an Apostle. The disciples had been asked to wait in Jerusalem until they should be endued with power, but at the time of the appointment of Matthias they had not been so endued; they therefore seem to have acted without power or authority. Besides, the Lord Himself afterwards appeared and commissioned another. Now, if Matthias really was an Apostle, there must have been thirteen. But this conflicts with at least two passages of Scripture. Christ says, speaking of the Apostles, "Ye which have followed me, in the regeneration when the Son of Man shall sit in the throne of His glory, ye also shall sit upon *twelve* thrones judging the twelve tribes of Israel."‡ We are also told that in the foundations of the "holy Jerusalem" twelve in number "are the names of the twelve apostles of the Lamb."§ Which of the thirteen is unprovided for? we think it must be Matthias.

We have thus far found four indispensable qualifications of the Apostle, but if we had only succeeded in

---

* Acts i, 24.

† Most unquestionably the lot was decided by God. If the present appointment was to stand, it was He who decided that Matthias should have the appointment; if it was not to stand, then He decided only this, that the delusive hope unwarrantably held out by the Apostles should fall to Matthias.

‡ Matt. xix, 28. § Rev. xxi, 14.

showing that one of these was necessary to constitute such an officer, we would have shown conclusively that he does not now exist.

In the second place, their work is perfect and complete, done once and for all. This follows from their qualifications. There are none now who have them, and therefore, there are none who can do their work, which is either complete, or God has left it unfinished and never to be finished, but such is not the case. God has finished the work in which they were engaged.

It follows from their work itself that such officers no longer exist. It was theirs to finish the writing of the Bible: that work is finished and perfect. It was theirs, from personal observation, to bear witness to the resurrection of Christ: the fact of the resurrection has been established beyond the possibility of doubt. It was theirs to work miracles as evidence of the truth of what they taught: the doctrines of Christianity have been shown to be as true as God Himself, and consequently, there is no further need of miracles. Doubly sure are we then that the Apostles were extraordinary officers, and have ceased.

As the prophet has nothing whatever to do with controversies on Church Government, I merely stop to say, that as he was one who taught by the inspiration of the Holy Ghost, he has ceased to exist in the Church, for the same reasons that Apostles have ceased, viz., his qualifications are not now possessed by any, and his work is completed.

The evangelist also, as such, has nothing to do with our controversy, but lest some should afterwards lay claim to him as a diocesan bishop, we now point out the nature of his work, and show that he has passed away. We do not show this to be a fact in precisely the same way as that by which we demonstrated that the Apostles were extraordinary officers, for we do not think that there was any qualification necessary for him, which may not be possessed by men now; but this holds in reference to him, his special work has been completed, and stands finished for all coming ages; which, as we have already seen, is abundantly sufficient to prove that he no longer exists. But while we endeavour to find out what his special work was, we shall find another reason to conclude that his office has ceased, viz., this, *the officers who alone could appoint him his work, and give him authority to do it, are themselves no more.*

What then was the special work of the evangelist? In establishing a Church in any place in primitive times, three things were required :—1st, the instruction of the people in the first principles of the Christian religion; 2nd, a form of Church Government—the way in which the ordinances of religion were to be preserved among them—needed to be shown them; and 3rd, they required a little superintendence until they became accustomed to the new order of things. The Apostles, doubtless, could do the whole of the above work, but it is also plain that much of it could be done by assistants; and, by employing such, the Apostles would be able to overtake much more work.

These assistants could go before the Apostles to prepare the way for them; travel with them to help them; or remain behind them, "to set in order the things that were wanting." We find that the Apostles did employ such assistants, and they were the evangelists. If asked to prove from Scripture that this was the work of the evangelist, we promise to do so before we leave this subject, but not now. But, if this position be admitted for the present, it follows that the work of the evangelist was a part of the Apostle's work, and the latter being finished, the former is also; further, it follows that the evangelists possessed extraordinary powers, in consequence of their being connected with the Apostles, who had an extraordinary commission and supernatural qualifications, *i. e.*, the evangelists were, so to speak, instruments in the hands of the Apostles, and as a matter of course, inasmuch as an instrument is of no use without the hand and skill to use it, when the Apostles passed away, the evangelists also passed away.

I need not mention the gifts of healing and diversities of tongues. They are, it is true, among the gifts given by Christ to the Church; but they do not come into Church Government at all, and besides, all such gifts have ceased. We have now remaining, pastors, teachers, and those signified by helps and governments. Out of these we must get the officers of the Church, in our day, as all others have passed away. There are other names by which those officers who remain in the Church are known, but no additional officer is specified.

OTHER NAMES FOR PASTORS, TEACHERS, HELPS, AND GOVERNMENTS.

We find that the ordinary church officers are known in Scripture by the following additional names, *elder* (πρεσβύτερος), bishop ('επίσκοπος), deacon (διάκονος), and besides these we do not find any other. But it may be asked, how can it be known that these are only other names for pastors, teachers, &c. We have abundance of proof to substantiate our statement. We are informed that "Paul sent to Ephesus, and called the elders of the church," and in the course of his address to them he said, "Take heed therefore unto yourselves, and to all the flock (ποιμνίῳ) * * * to feed (ποιμαίνειν, to perform the duties of a pastor to a flock), the church of God which he hath purchased with his own blood."* We see by this, that elders are to perform the duties of pastors to the flock. Again, he says to Timothy, "Let the elders that rule well be counted worthy of double honour, especially they who labour in the word and doctrine."† One who labours in word and doctrine is a teacher, and therefore an elder who labours in word and doctrine must be a teacher. Are pastors and teachers then, one

---

* Acts xx, 28. † 1 Tim. v, 17.

and the same? It would seem so, from the fact that an elder is both pastor and teacher, and also from the fact that Paul, in giving what appears to be a complete list, leaves out one of the names *(pastor)*, and in the other list he assigns to some the rank of apostles; to some that of prophets; to some that of evangelists; and to some that of pastors and teachers. By coupling *pastors* and *teachers* together, making them in the list of the same value as apostles, prophets, or evangelists, we take it that they were different names for the same officer.

Helps, whatever they may be, are neither pastors, teachers, nor governments, as the latter are separately mentioned; they neither teach nor rule, as there are special officers for the performance of these duties, viz., pastors (Heb. xiii, 7, 17; 1 Tim. v, 17) and governments. What, then, are their duties? There is nothing else that we know of, to be done in the Church, except such things as those for which deacons were appointed. The deacons, moreover, were appointed as helps to the Apostles, and yet not to assist them in either preaching or ruling; and further, Paul does not mention *deacons* in his lists of gifts to the Church, unless under the designation, *helps*, and so we conclude that *helps* and *deacons* are also different names for the same officers.

As to who are to be understood by *governments*, it does not affect our argument in any way at present; and, therefore, we ask the reader to allow us to leave the subject for a little, as we purpose taking it up in another chapter.

Church officers consist of only elders and deacons.

We have seen already that elders, bishops, and deacons are the same with pastors, teachers, and helps, and that these, with the exception of *governments* (reserved for future consideration), are all the officers to which the Church is in our day entitled. We may then proceed with elders, bishops, and deacons. These may be still further reduced. *Elder* and *bishop* are different names for the same officer. In that passage lately quoted from the Acts, Paul says to the *elders*, "Take heed therefore unto yourselves, and to all the flock over which the Holy Ghost hath made you *bishops* (*overseers* in the authorized version, but erroneously so, as the original is 'ἐπισκόπους, which has been everywhere else rendered *bishops*, and it is the only word so translated). The same fact also appears from the Epistle to Titus, chap. i, 5, 7. "For this cause left I thee in Crete, that thou shouldest set in order the things that are wanting, and ordain *elders* in every city, as I had appointed thee. If any be blameless, the husband of one wife, having faithful children, not accused of riot or unruly. For a *bishop* must be blameless." Here it is plain that the two words are used for the same officer, else why give as a reason for appointing the elders from those who are blameless (verse 6th), "a bishop must be blameless" (verse 7th)? We have now the two orders, viz., elders or bishops, and deacons. This harmonizes with the salutation of Paul and Timothy to the Church at Philippi, in which the saints, *i. e.*, ordinary church members and church officers are addressed, and the latter are spoken of as "bishops and deacons."* Again, Paul gives Timothy directions as to the ordering of the Church, and, among other things, he tells him of the qualifications necessary for church officers, and of these, he mentions but two orders, viz., bishops and deacons.†

The deacons do not preach the word, or administer the sacraments; but they have, as their department, the care of the contributions of the Church, and the oversight of the poor of the congregation as to their temporal necessities. This is proved by the following passage of Scripture, "In those days, when the number of the disciples was multiplied, there arose a murmuring of the Grecians against the Hebrews, because their widows were neglected in the daily ministration. Then the twelve called the multitude of the disciples unto them, and said,

---

* Phil. i, 1.   † 1 Tim. iii, 1-13.

It is not reason that we should leave the Word of God, and serve tables. Wherefore, brethren, look ye out among you seven men of honest report, full of the Holy Ghost and wisdom, whom we may appoint over this business. But we will give ourselves continually to prayer and to the ministry of the word."* There now remains but one order, elders or bishops, hence we conclude that *there is but one order in the Ministry.*

We have thus far endeavoured to develop the system of Church Government taught in the Scriptures; we are well aware, however, that others, who also profess to take the Bible for their guide in this matter, have arrived at conclusions widely different from ours. We shall now undertake to defend our doctrine, of *one order in the Ministry*, against our only opponents, the Episcopalians.

EPISCOPALIAN ARGUMENTS AND OBJECTIONS ANSWERED.

Some of the most learned and able Prelatists have conceded the point, that the scriptural bishop is the same with elder or presbyter, and different from diocesan bishop or prelate. Dean Alford, in his comment upon Acts xx, 17. says: "τοὺς πρεσβυτέρους called ver. 28, ἐπισκόπους. This circumstance," viz., the calling of τοὺς πρεσβυτέρους (the elders) ἐπισκόπους (bishops) "began very early to contradict the growing views of the apostolic institution and necessity of prelatical episcopacy." Immediately following these words he gives a quotation from Irenæus, showing how the latter perverts Scripture to teach his own views. Here is the quotation: "In Mileto convocatis episcopis et presbyteris, qui erant ab Epheso et a reliquis proximis civitatibus."† Upon this quotation he remarks:—"Here we see (1) the two, bishops and presbyters, distinguished, as if *both* were sent for, in

---

* Acts vi, 1-4.

†"The *bishops* and *presbyters* who were from Ephesus and the other neighbouring states, being assembled at Miletus."

order that the titles might not seem to belong to the same persons,—and (2) other neighbouring churches also brought in, in order that there might not seem to be ἐπίσκοποι in one church only. That neither of these was the case, is clearly shown by the plain words of this verse: he sent *to Ephesus* and *summoned the elders of the church.* So early did interested and disingenuous interpretations begin to cloud the light which Scripture might have thrown on ecclesiastical questions. The English version has hardly dealt fairly in this case with the sacred text, in rendering ἐπισκόπους, ver. 28, '*overseers;*' whereas it ought there, as in all other places, to have been *bishops* that the fact of *elders and bishops having been originally and apostolically synonymous* might be apparent to the ordinary English reader which now is not." Again in his comment on 1 Tim. iii, 1, he says: " But the ἐπίσκοποι (bishops) of the New Testament have officially nothing in common with our *bishops.* (See notes on Acts xx, 17, 28.) The identity of the ἐπίσκοπος (bishop) and πρεσβύτερος (elder or presbyter) is evident from Titus i, 5-7, see also note on Phil. i, 1." On Titus i, 7, " FOR IT BEHOVES AN OVERSEER," (translated in our Bible, *a bishop must be.*) He says, overseer, *i.e.*, bishop, is "here most plainly identified with the presbyter spoken of before." On Phil. i, 1, the same author quotes Theodoret to establish the same views as he had already given on the passages quoted above. The quotation from Theodoret is as follows: "ἐπισκόπους τοὺς πρεσβυτέρους καλεῖ· ἀμφότερα γὰρ εἶχον κατ' ἐκεῖνον τὸν καιρὸν ὀνόματα."* And Theodoret, on another of these passages, has words to the same effect.

Thus Alford holds precisely the same views as we do on every passage which we have quoted to prove the identity of the Scripture bishop and elder. It is refreshing to find one holding a high position in the Church of England, thus overcoming the prejudices of his denomi-

---

*He (that is Paul) calls bishops elders, for both the names, according to him, are equally appropriate.

nation, and declaring what is the plain teaching of inspiration on the matter. Nor is he alone among Episcopalians in these views. Ellicot, while he would gladly find hierarchical views in the Scriptures, and while he does actually try to do away with the force of what he says, is compelled to make the following acknowledgments: "Without entering into any discussion upon the origin of episcopacy generally, it seems proper to remark, that we must fairly acknowledge with Jerome, (Epist. 73, Vol. iv. p. 648,) that in the pastoral epistles the terms ἐπίσκοπος and πρεσβύτερος are applied indifferently to the same persons."*

We can hardly suppose that any intelligent man will maintain in the face of such clear evidence as we have produced to the contrary, that the primitive bishop and diocesan are the same; but if there are any who will, we shall labour no further to convince them. Where then is the diocesan to be found?

Where the Diocesan is sought.

He is supposed to be the successor of the Apostles; yet Prelatists do not believe that Apostles, as such, have successors. What is the explanation? Let Archbishop Whately answer: "As personal attendants on the Lord Jesus and witnesses of his resurrection—as dispensers of miraculous gifts—as inspired oracles of divine revelation —they have no successors. But as members, as ministers, as governors of Christian communities, their successors are the regularly admitted members, the lawfully ordained ministers, the regular and recognized governors of a regularly subsisting Christian Church."† We do not deny that the Apostles sometimes performed the duties of ordinary church officers, but we part company with the Prelatist here; he maintains that the Apostles, as ordinary officers, held a higher position than the primitive

---

* Ellicot on 1 Tim. iii, 1.   † Kingdom of Christ, p. 276.

bishop or elder; this we deny, and we are prepared to prove from the Scriptures, that, as ordinary officers, they were elders. If we succeed in doing this, the case for Prelacy is forever lost, for no one dares to contend that the primitive bishops were diocesans, and if it can be shown that the Apostles never held the prelatic office, the attempt to prove that Timothy, Titus, and Epaphroditus, their subordinates, were prelates, will be a vain one indeed.

The Apostles, as ordinary officers, were elders, not diocesans.

1. *Direct Scripture proof.*

That Church which is the mother of the Church of England, and from which the latter has inherited her entire system of Church Government, maintains that Peter was the chief of the Apostles; and the Papist certainly has more of the appearance of an argument both from Scripture and reason for this dogma, than the Church of England has for the headship of the Queen of England over those whom that Church professes to believe are the successors of the Apostles: and yet we venture to take the testimony of Peter as to his position, as an ordinary officer, in the Church. "The elders," says he, "which are among you I exhort, who am also an ELDER"[*] (lit., who am a fellow-elder). John was the beloved disciple. On more than one occasion Peter, James and he were specially honoured of the Lord, and yet John never rose as an ordinary officer above the dignity of the eldership, for thus he designates himself, the ELDER. "The *elder* unto the elect lady and her children;"[†] "The *elder* unto the well beloved Gaius."[‡] Paul "was not a whit behind the very chiefest apostles,"[§] and yet when the Holy Ghost directed

---

[*] 1 Pet. v, 1.   [†] 2 John 1.   [‡] 3 John 1.   [§] 2 Cor. xi, 5.

that Paul should be set apart to a certain work, the preaching of the gospel in certain parts (and whether the mission was temporary or otherwise it matters not, it was the work of an ordinary servant of the Church), he was ordained and set apart to that work by elders, and as they could not confer a higher ordination than their own, it follows that Paul, in doing that work, had only, in his ordinary capacity, the rank of an elder.*

The above passages are quite sufficient to prove that the Apostles were elders and not diocesans; nor can the contrary ever be established until they are removed from the Bible, and Peter, John, and Paul are made to declare that they were prelates.

But yet it may be satisfactory to some to show that this is just what might be expected from the general principles which Christ laid down for the guidance of His Apostles before he left this world. In speaking of the Pharisees, Christ said to His disciples: "They make broad their phylacteries, and enlarge the borders of their garments, and love the uppermost rooms at feasts, and the chief seats in the synagogues, and greetings in the markets, and to be called of men, Rabbi, Rabbi. But be not ye called Rabbi; for one is your master, even Chirst; and all ye are brethren. And call no man your father upon the earth; for one is your Father which is in heaven. Neither be ye called masters; for one is your master, even Christ. But he that is greatest among you shall be your servant."† Again, when the mother of Zebedee's children came to Jesus, and urged on by an unhallowed ambition, asked that her two sons might sit, the one on His right hand and the other on His left in His kingdom, and the ten were, naturally enough, moved with indignation on hearing such a request, He explained how things would be in His kingdom in these words: "Ye know that the princes of the

---

* Acts xiii, 1, 2, 3.   † Matth. xxiii, 5-11.

OF WHAT OFFICERS DOES THE MINISTRY CONSIST? 61

Gentiles exercise dominion over them, and they that are great exercise authority upon them. But it shall not be so among you: but whosoever will be great among you, let him be your minister; and whosoever will be chief among you, let him be your servant."* The only other directions which he gave to indicate the work of his servants, as church officers, amount to but two or three such as these, "Preach the Gospel to every creature," "Feed my lambs," "Feed my sheep," the first addressed to all the Apostles and the two last to Peter: these indicate, not the work of the diocesan who rules pastors and teachers, and too often lords it over God's heritage, but that of the humble pastor.

The above is so diametrically opposed to the hierarchical system of Church Government, that I wonder the author of "Our Church and Her Services" had the courage to refer to the "few" directions of our Lord, unless he thought them so few that his reader would not trouble himself about them. I would not willingly or wantonly hurt the feelings of any member of the Church of England; but yet I ask, if an unprejudiced man would not, if asked to guess, from what is the practice in that denomination, the direction which our Lord gave to the Apostles, frame something like the following: There are gradations of rank among civil rulers, and there ought to be the same among the spiritual. The position of a diocesan is higher than that of a priest, and a priest is superior to a deacon; hence if you are a deacon or priest strive to be a diocesan, that you may be the better able to do good by getting more power. The civil ruler will have power to give you a see; if you get the offer of it, take it, no matter how vehemently God's people may protest against your elevation. Be called of men, My Lord, My Lord, and if any of your own refuse you the title, assert your right to it; make them give it; and if those of another denomination, over which you have no power, refuse to

---

* Matth. xx, 25-27.

acknowledge you as their lord and master, call them unmannerly and uncourteous schismatics.

2. *The Practice of the Apostles.*

The practice of the Apostles shows that they were, as ordinary officers, elders or presbyters, and not diocesan bishops. The Apostles had no fixed field, but laboured in different places, sometimes singly, and at other times several of them in company. How was it with Paul, for example, was there anything in common between him and a diocesan with respect to a see? In performing his work, he travelled from Arabia to Rome, and perhaps as far as Spain, for he speaks of going there. Nor did he do this because his flock was in two places wide apart, for in every place where he stopped—in every place through which he passed—he preached the gospel. He had enough territory, one would think, to command an Œcumenical council, so if he belonged to the prelatical hierarchy he must have been pope. And indeed, Bishop Oxenden teaches that he was pope, for at page twelfth of "Our Church and Her Services," he says: "St. Paul speaks of himself as 'having the care of all the churches;' just as a bishop has in his diocese in the present day." What is this but to make a pope of Paul? Had he not the care of all the churches in Crete where Bishop Titus was, as well as in Ephesus where Bishop Timothy was, and in all other places where there were other supposed diocesans, and his authority over all these was precisely similar to that of a bishop in his diocese at the present day: the pope, as to the extent of his spiritual jurisdiction, and also as to the manner of exercising his power, claims no more. But let me say, that those, who maintain the supremacy of the pope, claim that high position for Peter. In so far I agree with the Episcopalians, that if either of them has a right to such supremacy, Paul is the man. But Paul was neither a pope nor yet a diocesan. As an Apostle, he travelled everywhere, and established the Christian Church according to the

OF WHAT OFFICERS DOES THE MINISTRY CONSIST? 63

pattern which the Lord had given him, convincing men that he had a divine commission by the "signs and wonders of an apostle;" and as an ordinary officer he preached the gospel just as a presbyter or primitive bishop.

Again, says the same author, "We gather from the Acts and from the Epistles, that St. James was appointed the first Bishop of Jerusalem."* Even though we could "gather" this supposed fact from the Acts and the Epistles, it would prove nothing for him, as a bishop and presbyter are one and the same. But perhaps he means to tell us that James was appointed the first diocesan of Jerusalem. If so, he must have made a great *gathering* such as no man before him has ever made. I wish he had told us what his several discoveries were. Why, there is not the shadow of proof that James was ever diocesan of Jerusalem, or of any other place, while there is much to show that he was not a diocesan at all. If he were the diocesan of Jerusalem, we ask how the dispute which arose in the church at Antioch came to be referred, not to James, but to the *Apostles* and *elders* at Jerusalem? If Apostles were diocesans, how did it happen that there were several in the one see, viz., Jerusalem? How was it, that it was the Apostles and elders with the whole Church who sent letters, and not his grace the bishop? What right would James have, as diocesan of Jerusalem, to enforce his decrees in Antioch? We cannot see how any one reading carefully the fifteenth chapter of the Acts can fail to gather from it this fact, that James was not diocesan of Jerusalem. The only expression in it likely to mislead a careless and ignorant reader is the one in the nineteenth verse: "Wherefore my sentence is;" but any one at all skilled in the interpretation of Scripture knows right well that this simply means, my opinion is, &c.

It will further be noticed, that the Apostles not only

---

* "Our Church and Her Services."

laboured in such a way as to show that they were not diocesan bishops, but on every occasion in which they acted as ordinary officers, they acted as elders or primitive bishops. The diocesan claims the exclusive right to ordain; the Apostles never ordained singly, but as members of a presbytery, which alone is said to ordain. There is not a solitary instance of an Apostle's laying his hands on any one's head to set him apart to the Ministry. We may be told here that Paul alone ordained Timothy, as it is said in the second Epistle to him: "Wherefore I put thee in remembrance, that thou stir up the gift of God which is in thee by the putting on of my hands."* After being informed that Timothy was ordained by the presbytery,† the most natural thing for us to do is to look for some other explanation of this passage; if such cannot be found, then it will be time enough to bring it into conflict with what is said in the first Epistle about the laying on of the hands of the presbytery. But there is nothing more easy than the explanation. The Apostles, by the laying on of their hands, had the power of imparting spiritual gifts,‡ and the reference in the passage is to such a gift, and not to ordination at all. Paul himself received such a gift at the hands of Ananias,§ but notwithstanding, Paul was ordained by the Presbytery of Antioch.‖ The language used in the Epistles to Timothy makes it clear that the first refers to ordination, and the second to a spiritual gift. Ordination sets apart to an office, and one may be pertinently told not to neglect an office, and to stir up a gift, but to stir up an office is nonsense.¶

In church courts the Apostles never assumed any superiority over the elders, but acted with them. In Acts xv, 6, it is said, "The apostles and elders came together to consider of this matter," and in the twenty-second verse of the same chapter it is said, "Then pleased it the apostles and elders with the whole church to send chosen

---

* 2 Tim. i. 6. † 1 Tim. iv, 14. ‡ Acts viii, 20. § Acts ix, 17.
‖ Acts xiii, 1, 2, 3. ¶ See "Plea of Presbytery."

men, &c." And so they did in all church courts. They call the elders their fellow-labourers and fellow-servants; they never took the oversight of the pastors, but always of the people. This, too, is just what we might expect, after what their Master had said to them. "Ye know that they which are accounted to rule over the Gentiles exercise lordship over them, and their great ones exercise authority upon them. But so it shall not be among you; but whosoever will be great among you shall be your minister, and whosoever of you will be the chiefest, shall be servant of all."* This was spoken immediately after the reproof of the two would-be lords of primitive times.

Let us now sum up what we have said in reference to the standing of the Apostles as ordinary officers:

1. The Saviour expressly forbade their taking to themselves prelatical power;
2. They distinctly said that they were elders;
3. There is not a single instance in the New Testament of their exercising prelatical power;
4. They did exercise the authority of elders on several occasions, and their whole bearing shows that this was all they ever claimed for themselves as ordinary ministers; and the attempt to establish the diocesan character of the Apostles is an ignominious failure.

Timothy, Titus, and Epaphroditus, not diocesans.

But since they would not accept the prelatic honour, some others must be found who did, or the cause of the Prelatist is lost. We fear it is already lost. The fact that the Apostles, who had, as extraordinary officers, the highest position in the Church, did not, as ordinary officers, accept or take a higher one than that of elder, and also, that they were forbidden to do so by the Saviour

---

* Mark x, 42, 43, 44.

Himself, makes it absolutely certain that they did not confer a higher honour upon any one else. But notwithstanding all this, it is affirmed by the Prelatist that Timothy, Titus, and Epaphroditus were diocesans. Now we know that it is quite possible for us to feel certain that our interpretation of Scripture is correct, and yet be mistaken; but nevertheless, when we build our judgment upon a great deal which we think very clear and conclusive, it must be something very plain and forcible indeed which can make us change our minds. We have a right then, to ask the most convincing proof of the prelatical standing of these worthies, before we can accept it as a fact. But what are the grounds upon which it is supposed that the prelacy of Timothy is established. Here they follow; let us mark them well:

1. He is forbidden to lay hands suddenly on any man. This shows that he alone had the right to ordain in his diocese.

2. He had a diocese, because Paul says to him, "I besought thee to abide still at Ephesus when I went into Macedonia."

I cannot forbear giving a sentence or two of Daillé here. "He besought Timothy to abide still at Ephesus. Here the hierarchs having their imagination full of their grand prelatures, of their bishopricks, and archbishopricks and their primacies do not fail to dream of one, in these words of the apostle, that '*he besought Timothy to abide still at Ephesus,*' and not only that but even make Timothy metroplitan or archbishop of the province, and even primate of all Asia. You see how ingenious is the passion for the crozier and the mitre, being able in so few and simple words to detect such great mysteries? For where is the man who in the use of his natural understanding, without being heated by a previous attachment, could ever have found so many *mitres*—that of a bishop, that of an archbishop, that of a primate, in those few words: '*Paul besought Timothy to abide still at Ephesus.*'

Who without the help of some extraordinary passion could ever have made so charming and so rare a discovery? and imagine that to beseech a man to stay in a city, means to establish him bishop of that city, archbishop of the province, and primate of all the country? In very deed, the cause of these gentlemen of the hierarchy must be reduced to an evil plight, since they are constrained to resort to such pitiful proofs."* "Who in the use of his natural understanding" could believe that the above fact establishes the prelatic standing of Timothy? However, while there is nothing to prove that Timothy was a prelate, we need not be at a loss to find out what he really was—he was an evangelist. Says Paul to him, "Do the work of an evangelist, make full proof of thy ministry."† We have already spoken of the duties of such an officer: he was an assistant to the Apostle and derived all his extraordinary power by his being so connected with that officer. Without the direction of the Apostle, the evangelist was just an ordinary minister. And as Timothy was ordained by a presbytery he must have been a presbyter. Now there is not a word in the whole of the first or second Epistle relating to his authority, which is not plain and easily understood, if we bear in mind Timothy's extraordinary power. In the time of Paul the Church was still without a great part of the New Testament, for he and others were engaged in writing it. As the different parts of it which he wrote were finished, he sent them to the different churches to be read to the people, as he could not have a large number prepared for circulation. What more natural than that he should address some of these letters to his assistants, that they might make the contents known to those to whom they spoke for the Apostles? Hence when he says to Timothy, "*Lay hands suddenly on no man,*" it is not to be considered a private message to him such as an archbishop

---

* Translation from Plea of Presbytery. † 2 Tim. iv, 5.

might now send to his diocesan, but a message from the Word of God, alike to Timothy and to all to whom it could apply to whom he should make it known. It was as though Paul had had the elders of Ephesus and his evangelist Timothy before him, and had said to them all: "*Lay hands suddenly on no man.*" How absurd it would be to argue that because Paul had said to Timothy: "Keep thyself pure,"* that he was therefore the only person in Ephesus who had any right to keep himself pure; and yet it has the same logical force which the argument from the laying on of hands has.

But suppose that the contents of the Epistle were for Timothy alone, we can still show that he was not the only person in Ephesus who had power to ordain; but, on the other hand, that he was one of a company (a presbytery) which ordained. To lay hands on without due consideration, and thereby to set apart unworthy persons, is to commit a sin, and against this sin Timothy is warned by the words, "Neither be partakers of other men's sins,"* *i.e.*, the sins of others who had ordained rashly. The command to Timothy clearly is, do not join with others in ordaining unsuitable persons. But who will venture to draw the conclusion from this, Timothy, you are to take the power of ordaining into your own hands. Nevertheless, we are not only asked to accept such conclusions as these, but to accept them in the face of such truths as we have established in reference to the Apostles.

Next, as to Timothy's diocese. It is no difficult matter to show that Timothy could not have been diocesan bishop of Ephesus. First, the fact that Paul besought him to abide there still, shows that he might have been expected to go elsewhere. But if he were a diocesan he must have been ignorant of his duty indeed, if he did not know that he ought to remain in his see. Secondly, he did not remain anywhere as a settled minister. In proof of this, I may here quote what has been

---

* 1 Tim. v, 22.

OF WHAT OFFICERS DOES THE MINISTRY CONSIST? 69

"gathered" by another* from the Acts and the Epistles: "We learn from Acts xvi, 1–12, that Timothy first came to Paul when he was at Derbe and Lystra, that they proceeded together through Phrygia, Galatia, Asia, Mysia, and last of all that he came to Philippi, where he abode with Paul. He appears afterwards to have been sent from Philippi to Corinth, there to engage in the work of the Lord.† After remaining there for a time he repaired again to Paul at Philippi, and there joined him in the second Epistle to the Corinthians, written in both their names, 2 Cor. i, 1. From the 19th verse it is evident that Timothy, before this second Epistle was written, had preached Jesus among the Corinthians by Paul's appointment. After this, Paul removing from Philippi, Timothy accompanied him to Thessalonica and Berea, where he abode till Paul came to Athens, from whence he sent a command to Timothy to Berea to come to him with all speed to Athens, where he stayed for him.‡ He joined with Paul in the first and second Epistles to the Thessalonians written from Athens in both their names.§ When Paul remained at Athens he sent Timothy to the Thessalonians to establish and comfort them concerning their faith. After continuing there for a short space he came again to Paul to Athens, bringing him good tidings of their faith and charity.‖ Then again he removed with Paul to Corinth. From this he was sent into Macedonia, and returned again to Paul at Corinth.¶ The Epistle to the Romans was written from this, and the Apostle remembers among others the salutation of Timothy, his workfellow, to them.** After this Paul, removing to Ephesus, sent Timothy into Macedonia,—himself staying in Asia for a season.†† If he had been a diocesan bishop surely the Apostle would not have sent him away from his see to interfere with the ministerial charges of others.

---

* Rev. Wm. McClure in the Plea of Presbytery.
† 1 Cor. iv, 17, xvi, 10. · ‡ Acts xvii, 13–16.   § 1 Thes. i, 1.,
2 Thes. i, 1, 2.   ‖ 1 Thes. iii, 1, 2.   ¶ Acts xix, 22.
** Rom. xvi, 21.   †† Acts xix, 27.

Paul afterwards passed into Macedonia and Greece, and then returned into Asia. Timothy and others accompanied him, and going before tarried for him at Troas.* This was after the Epistle to Timothy had been written, constituting him, as you suppose, sole bishop of Ephesus. The elders or bishops of that church were afterwards sent for and charged by the Apostle 'To take heed to themselves and to all the flock over which the Holy Ghost had made them *bishops*, to feed the Church of God which he had purchased, &c.'† If Timothy had been their diocesan it would have been much fitter for him to have delivered a charge to his own clergy. Of course we might expect that when Paul dismissed them, and they returned to Ephesus, that their diocesan would return along with them, and be doubly anxious to remain at home, and enforce obedience to the duties to which they were solemnly charged. But no; so far from going to Ephesus he accompanied Paul to Jerusalem.‡ From thence he went to Rome, for the Epistle to the Colossians written from that city bears both their names.§ He was in the same city when the Epistle to the Philippians was written, and from this, the Apostle intended shortly to send him to Philippi.|| He appears also to have been in bondage at Rome when the Epistle to the Hebrews was written, for his liberation is mentioned in Hebrews xiii, 23. The Epistle to the Hebrews was written from Italy, perhaps from Rome, about the end of Paul's imprisonment in that city. This was many years after the time he was supposed to be a settled diocesan. But what was his conduct after he was set at liberty? Does he immediately hasten to Ephesus, as we might expect, anxious to resume his charge and comfort the city so long in distress for a bishop? No. Utterly regardless of the affairs of his diocese, he made arrangements to proceed to Jerusalem, or possibly he went to Philippi, whither the

---

* Acts xx, 4, 5. † Acts xx, 28. ‡ Acts xxi, 15, 17.
§ Col. i, 1. || Phil. ii, 19.

Apostle had promised to send him. Thus Timothy appears to have been always attending the Apostle, or travelling by his appointment from one church to another." Much more might be said, many things might be produced in addition to what has already been brought forward to show that Timothy could not have been diocesan of Ephesus, nor yet a diocesan at all. We might notice such facts as the following. The Epistle to the Ephesians was written after the first to Timothy, which is supposed to have constituted him prelate, and yet in that Epistle not a word is said about the diocesan of Ephesus.

We have now shown not only that Timothy could not have been a diocesan, but we have also established beyond dispute his character as an evangelist—as an assistant to the Apostle, and we have now fully redeemed the promise which we made at the 52nd page.

We must now pass on to the case of Titus. He is supposed to be invested with prelatic dignity by these words, "For this cause left I thee in Crete, that thou shouldest set in order the things that are wanting, and ordain elders in every city, as I had appointed thee."* If it had been proved that the Apostles were diocesans, and that they never associated any with them when they ordained; if it had been proved that Timothy was a diocesan—in a word, if there were clear evidence that others were prelates,—then we might, at *first sight* conclude that Titus was created by Paul, diocesan of Crete; but when we have the words of the Saviour forbidding the Apostles to assume any such supremacy; when we see clearly by their practice that they could not have been prelates; when we have the express declarations of the Apostles that they were *elders*; when we find that Timothy, so far from being diocesan of Ephesus, was not a diocesan at all; but was, as an extraordinary officer, an evangelist who either travelled with Paul, or by his direction, and was, as an ordinary officer (being ordained by the presbytery) an

---

* Titus i, 5.

elder, we require something more than these words, "*I left thee in Crete to set in order the things that are wanting and ordain elders in every city, as I had appointed thee,*" to establish his diocesan character. First, the Prelatist must show that these words cannot be taken in any other sense than this, that *Titus was the only person in Crete who had power to ordain;* for if there were any other, he would also be diocesan according to Prelatists, and there would be no need of Titus. Secondly, he must show that if Titus did himself alone ordain, that it necessarily made a diocesan of him. If he fails to establish either of these, he entirely fails to carry his point. We ask the reader's attention to this point, because we are inclined to think that, in cases like the attempt to prove Titus a diocesan, many take that for proof which is no proof at all. It would not then make him a modern bishop if he alone performed this duty, except under certain circumstances, for we hold that there are other circumstances, in which not only one man may ordain and still be an elder, but in which a man may preach without ordination at all, and still be a properly accredited minister of the Lord Jesus. We hold also, that if Titus ordained alone, which is, as we shall see, exceedingly unlikely, that it was under these circumstances, and not under those in which a diocesan ordains.

It is unlikely that Titus ordained alone. The Cretians probably first heard of Christianity through those of their countrymen who were present when the Holy Ghost was poured out on the day of Pentecost,* nearly thirty years before the Epistle to Titus was written. That they had made some progress in Christianity, is evident from the directions which Paul gives to Titus as to the persons he should choose, not only Christian men, but those who had trained their children as Christians. There were also false teachers in Crete, as appears from chapter i, 14, 16, and iii, 9, 10. Under all these circumstances, there must

---

* Acts ii, 11.

have been true teachers, and probably some elders. If there were none, what was Paul himself doing before he left Titus? Is it possible that he who had Timothy ordained by the presbytery—who never ordained himself—would go and leave Titus alone without an elder in all Crete? No: he laboured diligently while with Titus, and left him to finish what he had begun. He had along with Titus and others no doubt ordained elders in some of the cities, and the direction to Titus was, have them ordained in all the cities. But how were they to be ordained; by Titus alone? No: "as I had appointed;" and how did Paul appoint such things to be done? Why, by a presbytery.

By the way it may be remarked here, that Titus was left to ordain according to Paul's appointment, bishops, for you perceive that at the 7th verse Paul calls this officer to be appointed a *bishop*; according to some Prelatists, Crete must soon have had enough diocesans. Titus, too, must have been an archbishop.

But apart altogether from the question of ordination, which we think entirely fails to establish what the Prelatist must establish to a certainty before his cause gains anything, viz., that Titus did actually ordain elders or bishops by the laying on of his hands alone, and which when established, must also be shown not to arise from a case of necessity, we can still show that Titus could not have been diocesan of Crete.

The Greek word ἀπέλιπον, translated *left*, in the 5th verse, means to leave only for a little while, and not to leave as a permanent minister, it is true the Textus Receptus has κατέλιπον, meaning to leave permanently, but it is not supported by manuscript authority. In support of what we have just said we give Alford's comment on *Titus*, i, 5. "For this reason I left thee behind (reff.) ἀπέλ, gives the mere fact of leaving behind when Paul left the island;—κατέλ would convey the idea of more permanence, (cf.) Acts xviii, 19, xxiv, 27. This difference may have occasioned the alteration of the reading from ecclesiastical motives, to represent Titus as permanent bishop of Crete." But in vain are the interpolations of zealous and unprincipled hierarchs. Paul sent for Titus, or intended to send for him very soon after leaving him, "When I shall send Artemas unto thee, or Tychicus, be diligent to come unto me to Nicopolis."* It was at this place that Alford thinks that Paul was taken prisoner and carried to Rome, where he wrote the second Epistle to Timothy. At all events it is certain from internal evidence that the second Epistle to Timothy was written after that to Titus, and in the former he tells Timothy that Titus has gone to Dalmatia.† Before this time it appears that he travelled and assisted the Apostle just as Timothy did.

Epaphroditus is claimed by some as a diocesan, because he is called "messenger,"‡ in the original ἀπόστολος, apostle. The twelve are called messengers or apostles by way of preëminence as those sent by Christ. He chose twelve whom he named messengers (apostles, *i. e.*, persons sent)§ ever after this they were called *the* Apostles. Whenever the word apostle or messenger is used in the New Testament in a sense different from that in which it is used when applied to the twelve, which happens only four times out of more than eighty cases, it is clearly defined whose the apostle is, as in the case under consideration, "your messenger." But who in his senses would say, that because one is called *your* messenger, it at once elevates him to the dignity of those who are called messengers by way of preëminence as being messengers of Christ? That argument is just as sensible which would go to show that one of Tennyson's heroines was Queen of England, because her companions crowned her Queen of May. To what a weak support will the dying strive to cling ! But even though it did show that Epaphroditus was an Apostle, it is one thing, as we have already seen,

---

* Titus iii, 12. † 2 Tim. iv, 10. ‡ Phil. ii, 25.
§ Luke vi, 13.

to be an Apostle; it is a quite different thing to be a diocesan.

The reader may think that we have given undue importance to the case of the three last mentioned, but we do it, not because of the intrinsic importance of the argument, but merely out of respect to what our adversaries please to call argument. This remark will apply to much of what follows on this part of the controversy.

The angels of the Seven Churches, not diocesans.

Thus far we have not, as we think, found any diocesans; but we have found clear evidence that those supposed to be such were presbyters or extraordinary officers who have passed away. But not so with Prelatists. They must suppose that some at least of the foregoing were of the hierarchy, or we could never account for their trying to press the facts which we are about to notice into their service, unless upon the principle which we have already hinted at, that one drowning catches hold of a straw. Say they 'The angels of the seven churches were prelates.' What they can possibly find anywhere to establish the above proposition, we are unable to comprehend. But what will men not discover when once they have invented a system, and afterwards determine to find it in the Bible. We can imagine them thus reasoning with themselves, John was commanded to address the angel of each church; now there must have been a great many ministers in each, and as only one was addressed, he must have been over all the others. We reject this, both for want of evidence, and because Scripture wars against it.

First, evidence is wanting. It must be proved that the word *angel* is used to mean only one officer. It is impossible to do this; on the contrary it can be shown from the usage of this author to mean more than one. He says, "I saw another angel fly in the midst of heaven, having the everlasting gospel to preach unto them that dwell on the earth, and to every nation, and kindred, and tongue, and people."* Here the whole company of those who publish the Word of God is represented by *one* angel.

But while the failure to prove the angel of the church *one* is disastrous to the argument of the Prelatist; on the other hand, provided it could be shown that only one person is signified, that one might be claimed, with a thousand fold more reason, by Presbyterians as the moderator of a session or presbytery of the church mentioned: for it is in the name of such an officer, that messages from the court over which he presides are sent forth, and through him the same court is addressed. Taking this along with what we already know in connection with church officers, and we greatly mistake, if the said angel does not more closely resemble a Presbyterian moderator than a diocesan.

Leaving the passages immediately under consideration, we shall find that the interpretation of the Prelatist is contrary to common sense as well as to Scripture. We have already seen that during the life of Paul there was no diocesan in Ephesus, or in any other place: the Church at Ephesus was governed by elders, either as a session or presbytery. Then according to the prelatic view of the passages in the Revelation, we must suppose that Paul, who did so much towards the establishment of the Church, left one of the most important things in Church Government to the last surviving Apostle, and that this last Apostle introduced it, without giving us a single hint of it, excepting the word angel in that difficult and mystical book the Revelation. But this Apostle, says the Prelatist, was himself a diocesan, and as he was sending messages to the prelates of the seven churches, he must, at least, have been—first among equals—an archbishop. But he tells us himself that he was an elder.

In concluding this part of our subject, we shall just

---

* Rev. xiv, 6.

notice one thing said to prove that the angel was a diocesan. It is written, "Thou hast tried them which say they are apostles, and are not, and hast found them liars."* This trial of the pretended apostles shows that he who tried them, viz., the angel addressed, was a prelate. A begging of the question indeed! elders have that power. Every Christian may demand of him who claims to be an apostle, the commission and signs of an apostle. This is surely trying them, and if it entitles one to prelatic dignity, we ourselves may, without I think overestimating our work, claim as a reward for it, a mitre.

No Argument in support of Prelacy from the Jewish Hierarchy.

Here the controversy with Prelatists properly speaking ends. They, however, contend that their system is supported by the case of the seventy sent out by Christ, and also by the Jewish Hierarchy. But these, belonging to another dispensation, can never be of any authority in ours. It is true that some things in the Jewish Church may be appealed to as an additional confirmation of things taught in the Christian Church, or Jewish practices may be followed where it is clearly indicated that they are to be our models; but such can only be the case where the end of the institution is moral and not typical. But what shall we say to those who, having failed altogether to find anything in the New Testament in support of their doctrines, appeal to what is *typical* in the old. Such examples can never establish their teaching. If every officer in the modern hierarchy was mentioned in the Jewish, and by name too, if the Old Testament gave the whole catalogue, pope, cardinal, archbishop, bishop, archdeacon, dean, vicar, rector, and deacon, it would not be any ground for establishing such a form of government in the New Testament dispensation. But granting that it is an authority, we

---

* Rev. ii, 2.

shall find that the Prelatist cannot by any means get his system out of it.

He tells us, it is true, that the officers of the Jewish dispensation are typical, but typical of the Christian ministry, *i. e.*, the high priest, priests, and Levites are typical of the modern bishops, priests, and deacons. But where is the parallel? The Episcopalian may tell us that the Levites of old represent the deacons of modern times; the priests of the Jewish hierarchy, those of the Episcopal; and a solitary high priest, all the archbishops and suffragans; methinks the churchman, as he proudly styles himself, must feel very doubtful about the parallel in the last mentioned particular. But he need not feel doubtful any longer, for not only is it no parallel in appearance, it is none in reality. The Bible draws the parallel. In the Epistle to the Hebrews we learn that the high priest was typical of the Lord Jesus Christ. "Wherefore in all things it behoved him to be made like unto his brethren, that he might be a merciful and faithful high priest in things pertaining to God, to make reconciliation for the sins of the people."* Again, in the first of the third chapter He is called, "the high priest of our profession." We need not add more here to prove that Christ is the anti-type of the high priest, the fact is so well understood, though very much more might be produced. We shall also find too, that the *priests*, under the old dispensation, were typical of believers under the new. Says the Spirit by John, "Thou" (the Lamb) "art worthy to take the book, and to open the seals thereof; for thou wast slain, and hast redeemed us to God by thy blood out of every kindred, and tongue, and people, and nation; and hast made us unto our God kings and priests."† The Levites, instead of being typical of the third order of a ministry, were, if typical of anything, we should say, typical of the whole Ministry; and we are fully persuaded that we can carry out this parallel with a fair show of reason on our

---

* Heb. ii, 17. † Rev. v, 9, 10.

OF WHAT OFFICERS DOES THE MINISTRY CONSIST? 81

The twelve were sent forth two by two. "And He called unto Him the twelve, and began to send them forth by two and two."*

So were the seventy; "And sent them two and two before His face."‖

The twelve were sent forth in the most dangerous circumstances, as sheep among wolves. "Behold, I send you forth as sheep in the midst of wolves; be ye, therefore, wise as serpents, and harmless as doves."†

So were the seventy; "Go your ways: behold I send you forth as lambs among wolves."¶

The twelve had their commission to preach the kingdom of heaven is at hand. "And as you go preach, saying, The kingdom of heaven is at hand."‡

So had the seventy; "And heal the sick that are therein, and say unto them, The kingdom of heaven is come nigh unto you."**

The twelve had the power to work miracles. "Heal the sick, cleanse the lepers, raise the dead, cast out devils; freely ye have received, freely give."§

So had the seventy; "And the seventy returned again with joy, saying, Lord, even the devils are subject unto us through thy name * * Behold, I give unto you power to tread on serpents and scorpions, and over all the power of the enemy, and nothing shall by any means hurt you."††

The twelve were sent forth with the authority of their Master, and in His name. "He that receiveth you re-

So were the seventy; "He that heareth you heareth me; and he that despiseth you despiseth me; and he

---

* Mark vi, 7.   † Matt. x, 16.   ‡ Matt. x, 7.   § Matt. x, 8.
‖ Luke x, 1.   ¶ Luke x, 3.   ** Luke x, 9.
†† Luke x, 17, 19.

F

ceiveth me; and he that receiveth me receiveth Him that sent me." *

that despiseth me despiseth Him that sent me." †

There is not a syllable anywhere in the Bible to prove that the twelve had any authority over the seventy, in as far as these missions were concerned, and Prelacy can gain absolutely nothing from this case. Indeed, we may well wonder how any could be so obtuse or infatuated as to bring it up. The same might be said of some other Episcopalian arguments which we have noticed. Why notice them at all, it may be asked; for two reasons, first, because the adversary who uses them may, by constant repetition, come to actually think them arguments worthy the name, and may even suppose, or try to make others believe, if we passed them by, that we did so, because we were unable to answer them. Secondly, there is no better way of exposing a bad cause, than by just showing the rottenness of that by which it is supported; for it is certain that he who has the right need not resort to such miserable proofs for its support.

Elders, according to the Scriptures, can do all that diocesans have a right to do, and there is therefore no need of the latter.

The following facts cannot be disputed:—it is the duty of elders to ordain. It was the elders who set apart Paul and Barnabas, it was the elders who ordained Timothy, and it was the Apostles acting as elders (as we have already seen) who ordained the seven deacons.

The elders rule. "Let the elders that *rule* well, be counted worthy of double honour."

What more can diocesans do? They can confirm, and confirmation is an invention of men; they can sit in parliament, and, as ecclesiastical rulers, they have no right to.

---

* Matt. x, 40.   † Luke x, 16.

What need is there then for diocesans? There are Churches which, according to the directions of Scripture, have only elders and rulers, and they are more successful in doing the work of the Lord, than Episcopal Churches. Why not abolish Episcopacy? It would hurt human pride and ambition; but it would liberate the Church of God, still in fetters through its existence.

CHAPTER IV.

GOVERNMENTS.

THE reader will bear in mind that we have already established the following points :— After showing what constitutes the Church, we next proved that her King and Head has given her a Ministry; in the third place we established the fact, that there is but one order in the Ministry. We have also replied to the objections both of those who contend that there should be no Ministry, or one of such a peculiar kind as to come to virtually the same thing; and of those who take the opposite extreme, and endeavour to establish a hierarchy, which is clearly opposed to Scripture and the liberty of God's people. We now take up the subject of "Governments."

The question meets us at the outset,

WHO ARE TO BE UNDERSTOOD BY GOVERNMENTS?

Not pastors and teachers, as these have already been mentioned in the list; not deacons, for they do not rule, and moreover are mentioned already under the name of *helps;* not elders or primitive bishops, who teach and administer the sacraments, for they are just pastors and teachers, as we have already proved; not diocesan bishops, for the Scripture knows nothing of such an officer: and even though it could be shown that the Apostles have diocesan bishops for their successors, still we could not infer that these are to be understood by *governments*, as they would in such circumstances be marked out in Paul's list by the designation, *Apostles.* Nor can we suppose that civil rulers are meant, for governments are given to the Church, and civil rulers have no authority in it, as we shall hereafter show. We are then shut up to the conclusion, that by *governments* is meant ecclesiastical officers, whose special duty it is to rule. In this view we are confirmed by another passage. Paul, in speaking of the different gifts bestowed on different persons, exhorts each to do that for which he is qualified, and among those so gifted, he mentions one who rules, that is, who only rules, as he speaks of other duties as being performed by others. " Having then gifts differing according to the grace that is given to us, whether prophecy, let us prophesy according to the proportion of faith; or ministry, let us wait on our ministering; or he that teacheth on teaching; or he that exhorteth on exhortation; he that giveth, let him do it with simplicity; *he that ruleth,* with diligence, &c."*

Nor are they the only rulers in the Church; the elders all rule. (I. Tim. v, 17.) Nor are they superior to the elders, for there is not a word in Scripture to indicate such a state of things, but on the contrary much which is opposed to it; neither is there anything to show that they are subordinate to the elders: there is then only one remaining supposition possible, and that is, that they are officers who rule in conjunction with the elders. This will appear all the more likely, when we come to consider the way in which ecclesiastical officers exercise their power, viz., not as individuals but as members of an assembly.

In the way indicated above, we see provision made for a state of things which is now approved, even by those

---

* Rom. xii, 6-8.

who at the first strenuously opposed it. Both Independents and Episcopalians were at one time opposed to any one's being associated with the clergy in the government of the Church, and both now begin to think it desirable. In one, at least, of the most influential Independent churches in Canada, the congregation is governed, not by the minister alone, but by him and a staff of officers chosen from the congregation. The Episcopal Church has oftentimes found great difficulty for want of such officers, and where she has been liberated from civil bondage, she has taken various means of avoiding the difficulty. In one way or another, she has been obliged to allow the laity, as she terms the private members of the Church, a representation, the allowing of which is but a confession on her part, that such officers are not only desirable, but indispensible.

We have hitherto refrained from giving a name to these officers, though we are aware that some denominations have done so. We have followed this course for two reasons : first, to show that it is not a name which we contend for, but an office ; and secondly, we did not wish to commit ourselves to any theory respecting the dignity of the office, until we had produced Scripture authority for it. We have now however, come to that point, where we may take up the theory of the Presbyterian Church on this subject. She holds that the officers indicated by the term *governments*, are elders whose special duty it is to rule. With this theory let us proceed.

THE RULING ELDERSHIP.

The Presbyterian Church has all along maintained, that there are two classes of elders, not differing as to rank or dignity, but solely in respect to official duty. The former class both preaches and administers the sacraments, and also rules ; while the latter only rules : she considers the ruling elders to be the officers signified by *governments*. It will at once be perceived, that by holding this doctrine and carrying it out in practice, there is, in reality, no change made in the constitution of the Church, except in giving a name to the latter, and in setting them apart to their special work by the ceremony of ordination.

The question then, whether the Presbyterian Church has here erred, is not one of vital importance; she contends most strenuously for the officer; but she is disposed to allow great liberty of opinion as to his official dignity.

But has she erred, and if so, where is the proof; is there evidence sufficient to convict her; or must she be allowed the benefit of a doubt; or can she be triumphantly vindicated?

Let Dr. P. C. Campbell be counsel for the prosecution, and let him now call his witnesses and examine them; (he has done so in his "Theory of the Ruling Eldership,") and we, as counsel for the defence, shall cross-examine his witnesses, and call on our own, so as to lay the whole case before our readers, who will kindly act as the jury.

At the outset he brings forward the Scriptures, and a better witness he could not possibly have. Scripture, says he, "warrants the admission of the laity to a place in the government of the Church." Again, 'it teaches that all elders are bishops, and that a bishop should be apt to teach, and therefore all elders should be apt to teach, and since they should all be apt to teach, it is intended that they should all be pastors or preachers of the Word as well as rulers.' Another witness, early history, not nearly so reliable as the first, "speaks of a class of lay rulers, *seniores*, but not of ruling elders." These are all the points of importance which he discusses.

At the very outset, we have to record an objection. He says: "Scripture warrants the admission of the laity to a place in the government of the Church." He will tell us at *once*, that he does not contend for the use of the term *laity*, except, for convenience sake, to distinguish the private members of the Church from the pastors. Nor are we disposed to quarrel with names; but with the fallacies lurking under them, we are very much disposed to quarrel. Dr. Campbell may say, if you dislike the terms *clergy* and *laity* (and we do dislike them most heartily), let us say *pastors* and *private members*, or ministers and people, and may add, Scripture warrants the admission of the people to a place in the government of the Church, but this in no way removes the fallacy which lurks under his statement. He proceeds upon the implied assumptions that the Church is composed of two distinct bodies, viz., a body of private members or laymen and a body of clergymen; that the interests of the two bodies are distinct, and that if the ministers appoint all the rulers, they will rule in the interests of the body appointing them, therefore the laity, to get justice, must also have representatives in the governing body. It may be thought that I have gone too far in giving what appears to be Dr. Campbell's views. But unless such things as I have stated, are implied in his teaching, the statement, "Scripture warrants the admission of the laity, &c.," has no force at all for the very purpose for which he makes it. Besides, what I have here set forth as implied in his statement, he makes explicit in the discussion of his subject. But the above is not at all the scriptural view of the Church. The Church is but one body, and all its members have a common interest. She possesses the power to organize herself in accordance with Scripture, where organization has been lost, or to continue her organization in accordance with Scripture, where it has not been lost, in virtue of her union with Christ. Every officer then appointed by her, whether a minister or what Dr. C. calls a *lay ruler*, is one appointed by the whole body of believers,* and, when so appointed, ceases to be a private member, and becomes a public servant or official. Lay ruler then, involves the same contradiction, as is implied in one's being, at the same time, a private and a public officer in the same society. "With good reason," says

---

* Ministers are appointed by the whole Church, chapter II.

Dr. Campbell, "might Vitringa complain of the misleading influence of an existing order of things on our minds in the reading of the Scriptures," and we heartily endorse the remark. We then reject the statement that Scripture warrants the admission of the laity to a place in the government of the Church, and lay down the following instead: Scripture warrants the Church to appoint other rulers in addition to the ministers for her government.

We next take up the testimony of early history. "It speaks," says Dr. C., "of a class of lay rulers, *seniores*, but not of ruling elders." He quotes the following passage from Hilary, " Old age is honourable among all nations; whence it is that the synagogue and afterwards the Church had seniors without whose counsel nothing was done in the Church; which by what negligence it grew into disuse I know not, unless, perhaps, through the indolence or rather pride of the doctors, while they alone wished to appear something." Upon this he remarks: " If from this passage, Presbyterian writers have endeavoured successfully, as is admitted by many learned men of other churches, to prove the existence in ancient times of a class of councillors resembling our lay assessors, their opponents might with equal success, have contended from it against the application to these councillors of the term presbyter."

But we think that their opponents could not, with equal success, have contended against the application of the name *presbyter* to these councillors. We know the result of the pride of the elders. There was a struggling among them as to who should be the greatest, and in due time we had the diocesan, metropolitan, patriarch, and finally, a pope. The same struggling which raised some to such a high position, crushed out altogether the seniors. But does not this suggest, that the degradation of the seniors began at an earlier period? We do not suppose that they were removed by one sweeping decree; but first their dignity was taken away (the elders who aspired to such high things would not be able to endure the thought that these humble rulers were of the same rank as themselves), and once the dignity was gone, it would not take long to forget the office altogether. Now while a single vestige of an office disappearing, confirms the Scripture proof of such an office, it does not follow that one can contend " with equal success," that the few remaining duties of an office or the remaining dignity of the office are all that ever pertained to it.

Suppose that two travellers from the torrid zone, unacquainted with our climate, and like a certain prince of whom we read, unbelievers in the possibility of the existence of ice or snow, were to visit us in the month of April. One picks up a newspaper, and in it, sees something which implies that the ground not long before was covered with snow. "This is all false," he exclaims ; " but it may have been the case," suggests the other, " for there is a small patch still covered with it ; another, which was covered yesterday, is all bare to-day." One of these travellers, upon the authority of the newspaper along with the confirmatory evidence of the patches of snow still remaining, maintains that the ground was not long ago entirely covered ; the other, in opposition to the paper, contends that there never was any more than the pieces which he sees. We hardly think that Dr. Campbell would say, that the latter maintains his position with the same success as the former. But even though he might, we cannot, neither can we say that the opponents of the ruling eldership contend against it, on the ground of early history, with the same success as those who uphold that theory, for the different positions taken by the travellers in our illustration are precisely those occupied by the two parties in the dispute about the seniors. The one says, the Bible teaches that there should be ruling elders, and that the existence of seniors, in an age which tended to the destruction of their office, confirms the teaching of the Scripture ; the other, that these seniors never had a higher dignity.

We now come to Dr. Campbell's strongest objection to the theory of the ruling eldership. We confess that it is an objection of some weight, and should be carefully considered. It is the only one of the kind in his book, and his production would have been much more forcible than it is, had he confined himself to it alone. It is as follows: 'All elders are bishops, and as a bishop should be apt to teach, all elders should be apt to teach, hence it is inferred that all elders are ministers of the Word.'

We leave this objection, until we have considered what there is to be said on the other side.

The Presbyterian Church has hitherto maintained, that those who are meant by *governments*, and who, we found, rule in conjunction with the ministers of the Word, are, like the ministers, elders; the difference being that they do not preach and administer the sacraments, but simply rule. She has founded this doctrine upon the well known passage in the First Epistle to Timothy, "Let the elders that rule well be counted worthy of double honour, especially they who labour in the word and doctrine."*

If she has erred in her inference from this passage, that there are two classes of elders, viz., one which rules; while the other both rules and labours in the Word and doctrine, she has erred in company with many learned men of other churches. Dr. Whittaker, a regius professor of theology in Cambridge, says, " By these words the apostle evidently distinguishes between the bishops and inspectors of the church. If all who rule well are worthy of double honour, especially they who labour in the word and doctrine, it is plain that there were some who did not so labour; for if all had been of this description the meaning would have been absurd; but the word, *especially*, points out a difference. If I should say that all who study well at the university are worthy of double honour, especially they who labour in the study of theology, I must either mean that all do not apply themselves to the study of theology, or I should speak nonsense. Wherefore I confess that to be the most

---

* I Tim. v, 17.

genuine sense, by which pastors and teachers are distinguished from those who only govern." Dr. Lightfoot, in his remarks upon First Timothy says, "He (Paul) prescribeth rules and qualifications for the choosing of an elder. He speaketh of elders ruling only and elders ruling and labouring in the word and doctrine." Fell, Bishop of Oxford, says, "Paul is seen to have distinguished formerly between those presbyters who were *rulers* and *doctors*. Dr. Whitby says, "The elders who were among the Jews were of two sorts: 1st, such as governed in the synagogue; and 2nd, such as ministered in reading and expounding the Scriptures * * * * Accordingly the apostle, reckoning up the offices God had appointed in the Church, places teachers before governments." Dr. Fulke of Cambridge, says, "Else he (Paul) meaneth of those elders that Saint Ambrose speaketh of upon the first verse of this chapter, that were appointed only for government and not for teaching." Archbishop Potter says in his work on Church Government, "Lastly there are teaching presbyters (doctors) spoken of in several other churches by way of distinction from other presbyters who did not exercise this office of public teaching."

Of Independents, Owen says, "On the first proposal of this text that the elders that rule well are worthy of double honour, especially those who labour in word and doctrine, a rational man who is unprejudiced, who never heard of the controversy about ruling elders, can hardly avoid an apprehension that there are two sorts of elders, some that labour in the word and doctrine, and some who do not so do. The truth is, it was interest and prejudice that first caused some learned men to strain their wits to find out evasions from the evidence of this testimony. Being so found out, some others of meaner abilities have been entangled by them." Dodderidge, in his commentary on this passage, says, that it teaches "that there were some who, though they presided in the church, were not employed in preaching." Dwight, speaking of this text, says, "Here St. Paul directs that preaching elders should be accounted worthy of more honour than ruling elders. As the elders are here supposed to rule well, that is, to do their duty faithfully, it is clear that the superior honour given to those who preach is given only on account of the superiority of their employment."*

Dr. Campbell may tell us that it is very disingenuous to quote Episcopal authorities in this connection, as they do not mean to teach that the elders who only rule have not authority to preach if they choose. We know it right well, but we quote them to show that they understand the text as teaching a distinction between the elders as to the duties which they perform, and not, as he would interpret it, by founding the distinction upon the manner in which they perform the same duties. But in the case of the authorities from the ranks of the Independents, he cannot make even this weak objection. It would seem then, that it is not without some show of authority that the Presbyterian Church has adopted the theory of the ruling eldership.

But Dr. Campbell rejects the above interpretation, and gives the following instead: "Let the presbyters who preside well be counted worthy of double recompense, especially they who are laborious in preaching and teaching." If this were a satisfactory explanation of the passage, we would accept it at once, but after carefully considering the matter we are obliged to reject it. The Greek word, rendered in the English Version *labour*, is here translated *are laborious*. Whatever may be said of the merits of this interpretation on other grounds, we think Dr. C. has departed from the New-Testament meaning of this word, and certainly from the sense in which Paul uses it. It occurs, if we mistake not, twenty-three times in the New Testament, fourteen times in the Epistles of Paul, and

---

* The above quotations are given on the authority of the PLEA OF PRESBYTERY.

nine in the Gospels, Acts, and the Revelation. Let us now examine some of these passages. Christ says of the lilies, "They toil (labour) not;"* this surely does not mean that the lilies are not laborious, for that would imply that they do work moderately. Paul says, "Greet Mary who bestowed much labour on us,"† and again, "Salute the beloved Persis which laboured much (*was laborious much* would not do very well) in the Lord."‡ If the word here means laborious, there is no need of the *much*. In one of the Epistles to Timothy it is said: "The husbandman that laboureth must be first partaker of the fruits,"§ but if he only work moderately, what then?

These examples clearly show that ordinary labour is intended; and in none of the twenty-three passages can it be shown that anything more is intended. We shall now take, as an example, one which an opponent would at once seize upon, and the only one out of the twenty-three, which has an appearance of the *laborious* in it. Christ says, "Come unto me all ye that labour and are heavy laden, and I will give you rest."‖ In the word *labour* here, is sin compared to ordinary labour which produces weariness, or to laborious toiling? We should say to the former, for the latter notion is better expressed by the words, *heavy laden;* and further, if it is only those who feel sin to be severe labour that are invited, then the invitation is narrowed, but we think it invites all who have discovered that sin is not pleasure, but continuous work, as well as those who have found its burdens heavy indeed.

The rendering of our English Version, we consider preferable, and the plain meaning of that is, that *some elders only rule, while others both rule and preach.* Taking this interpretation, which makes ruling the whole duty of some elders, we can understand why they should have double honour or double recompense, if they

---

* Matth. vi, 28.   † Rom. xvi, 6.   ‡ Ibid. xvi, 12.
§ II. Tim. ii, 6.   ‖ Matth. xi, 28.

perform that duty well, and we can also understand how especial honour should be given to those who have greater duties to perform, and also perform them well. But taking Dr. C's rendering, we cannot understand why Paul should say, that an elder who only performed part of his duty well, and that the smallest part, should have double recompense, while those who performed the whole well should having nothing more, except an especial mention. Here is a man, let us say, set apart to the office of the ministry (and Paul describes the ordinary work of this office by the term, *labour*, used in the text); who does not *labour* at all in his most important sphere, but according to Dr. C., merely conducts the meeting well of which he is the chairman; let him have double recompense, says Paul, for the little that he has done. We cannot accept such an interpretation.

Besides the passage which we have just considered, there are several other things which, we think, go to show that the theory of the ruling eldership is the correct one in reference to the *governments*.

1. We have directions as to the formal setting apart of both elders and deacons to their office, but no warrant, either direct or implied, for the setting apart of other rulers. It is reasonable to suppose that the *governments*, since their work is of as much, if not of more, account than that of the deacons, should be as solemnly set apart; but if they are not elders, not only is there no form given by which they are to be set apart, but no direction any where to appoint them in any way.

2. When Paul wrote to the Philippians, he addressed all the Saints, *i. e.*, all the private members of the Church, along with the *bishops* and *deacons*. Why did he not mention the *governments*, if not because they were included in the term *bishops*? Surely they were officers as deserving of notice as the deacons. He also wrote to Timothy, giving him directions as to the qualifications necessary in bishops and deacons, but says nothing of governments. Why, we ask, if not because they were among the bishops?

In early history, we frequently find that the officers of the Church were addressed, or spoken of by the same terms, bishops and deacons. How was it that the governments were so generally ignored, was it not because they were bishops?

We have now to consider the great objection to the theory of the ruling eldership noticed before, viz., *an elder is a bishop, and a bishop should be* apt to teach. This objection is of force, and it is the only one of any force against that theory. But we have seen that there are objections on the other side, and we must endeavour to reconcile them.

Aptitude for teaching does not of itself make one a preacher. There are many who possess it who could not preach at all. A Sabbath school teacher may be apt to teach; a father in his family may be apt to teach; a mother as she helps her child in his first lessons may be apt to teach; but yet none of the above may be qualified for preaching. Many in the Church besides the ministers of the Word should have aptitude for teaching. All Sabbath school teachers and Bible class teachers should have it, and what is more, all rulers in the Church should have it. We feel that we need teaching in various ways from those who are associated with the minister in ruling the congregation. The services of such persons are needed in visiting the sick, for conducting prayer meetings and such like; and all of these things require aptitude for teaching. Further, it is very questionable whether they can properly perform what none will deny are their own peculiar duties without such aptitude. Along with the minister, they assist at the communion, they put the bread and wine into the communicants' hands; just suppose then, that after the celebration of this ordinance, some spectator were to ask one of them "What mean you by this ordinance?" the confused ruler either through ignorance, or want of power to explain, cannot tell: might not the astonished enquirer exclaim, " Art thou a master of Israel, and knowest not these things?"

The Presbyterian Church directs the rulers of congregations to deal in the following manner with those under suspension. "While under suspension the individual ought to be the object of peculiar solicitude and care on the part of the rulers of the Church. Every seasonable opportunity of dealing with his conscience, impressing him with right views of his sin, and leading him to repentance should be diligently improved by them." No one reading this will say, that this Church has, in this matter, directed amiss. Now, to perform the duties spoken of above, precisely that patience and aptitude for teaching spoken of by Paul are required.

Dr. C. has another objection so like the one we have just been discussing that it needs no separate consideration. We just mention it here however, to show how it is met by the above. In the passage, quoted, some pages back, from the Acts, Paul shows the elders that it is their duty to feed, as a shepherd the flock. The ruling elder who performs his duty as indicated above, does his share of feeding it.

To sum up : 1. We hold by the passage in the Epistle to Timothy as it stands in the English Version, and the plain meaning is, that there are two classes of elders.

2. Only two orders are mentioned as the officers of the Church at Philippi, viz., bishops and deacons, and Paul in telling Timothy what the character of Church officers should be, &c., only mentions the bishop and the deacon.

3. We have particular forms for setting apart bishops and deacons to their respective offices, but no hint is given as to the way in which the supposed *lay* ruler should be set apart. This is unaccountable on the supposition of the existence of such an officer, as his work is of more account, we should naturally think, than that of the deacon.

The passage from Timothy, Dr. C. has tried to explain in harmony with his view, with what success the reader

G

may judge: he has not, however, noticed the remaining points which we have just brought forward. Besides answering Dr. C's other objections, we have tried to explain "apt to teach" in accordance with our view. Here we leave the case with the reader to give the verdict as he pleases. We think it a matter where our Church has wisely allowed liberty of opinion; but our own impression is that the theory of the ruling eldership is the correct one.

CHAPTER V.

THE DIACONATE.

THE deacon, as we have already seen, is recognized by Scripture as an ecclesiastical officer to whom it belongs to look after the poor, and other temporal matters connected with the Church. He neither preaches the Word nor administers the sacraments. The following passage sufficiently defines his duty, as well as shows how he is to be elected and set apart to his office. "In those days, when the number of the disciples was multiplied, there arose a murmuring of the Grecians against the Hebrews, because their widows were neglected in the daily ministration. Then the twelve called the multitude of the disciples unto them, and said, It is not reason that we should leave the Word of God, and serve tables. Wherefore, brethren, look ye out among you seven men of honest report, full of the Holy Ghost and wisdom, whom we may appoint over this business. But we will give ourselves continually to prayer, and to the ministry of the word. And the saying pleased the whole multitude; and they chose Stephen, a man full of faith and of the Holy Ghost, and Philip, &c.: whom they set before the apostles; and when they had prayed, they laid their hands on them."*

---

*Acts vi, 1–6.

We need not have any very lengthy controversy about the duties and position of deacons in the Church. Their duties are so clearly defined in the passage above quoted, that we well might wonder why different opinions were ever held concerning them, did we not know that men sometimes invent a doctrine, and afterwards come to the Bible to find support for it. The Prelatists, in their anxiety to bolster up their three orders, try to make it appear that deacons were ministers of the Word. They do not pretend that any such statement is made in Scripture, but they infer it from the fact, that some of the seven, appointed deacons, afterwards preached. But the inference is manifestly unfair and even childish. It does not follow that because a man is appointed to a particular office, that he must continue to discharge the duties of that office for his lifetime; he may surely resign it and take another. Hence it does not follow that Philip preached as a deacon. He is indeed afterwards mentioned by another name, viz., evangelist.*

Stephen, it is contended, preached.† Does it therefore follow that preaching was a duty connected with the office of deacon? Let us see. Suppose that in one of our Presbyterian churches, a certain man is appointed a deacon, and the same, or similar duties to those mentioned with reference to the seven in Acts, are pointed out to him as the duties of the office to which he has been elevated. The next day however, he is found among scoffers, ably arguing for the truth of Christianity. Are we to conclude that he was made a minister by the appointment of the previous day? The thing is absurd. He would be doing all that Stephen did, in the way of preaching, in arguing with the scoffers, and nothing more than any Christian might do,—nothing more than he might have done had he never been made a deacon.

Hooker, a great authority, if not *the* great authority among Episcopalians, with better grace, takes the position which Prelatists must take in this matter. He ad-

---

*Acts xxi, 8.   †Acts vi, 10.

mits frankly that the deacons were not originally teachers, and he was not the man to do so, if he could, by any appearance of plausibility, maintain the contrary. He says, "That the first seven deacons were chosen out of the seventy disciples, is an error in Epiphanius. For to draw men from places of weightier into rooms of meaner labour had not been fit. The apostles, to the end they might follow teaching with more freedom, committed the ministry of tables unto deacons. And shall we think they judged it expedient to choose so many out of those seventy to be *ministers unto tables*, when Christ himself had before made them *teachers?*"* "Deacons were stewards of the Church," says he, on another page, "unto whom, at the first, was committed the distribution of Church goods, the care of providing therewith for the poor, and the charge to see that all things of expense might be religiously and faithfully dealt in. A part, also, of their office was attendance upon their presbyters at the time of divine service." But how, according to Hooker, did they become ministers? "These only," (viz., things just enumerated) "being the uses for which deacons were first made, if the Church hath sithence extended their ministry farther than the circuit of their labour at the first was drawn, we are not herein to think the ordinance of Scripture violated, except there appear some prohibition which hath abridged the Church of that liberty." Again, after pointing out the reason given in the Acts for the appointment of deacons, he proceeds: "Now, tract of time having clear worn out those first occasions for which the deaconship was then most necessary, it might the better be *afterwards extended to other services*, and so remain as at this present day, a degree in the clergy of God, which the apostles of Christ did institute."

Hooker then honestly admits that Scripture does not teach that deacons are an order of preachers; but that

---

* Laws of Ecc. Pol., Book v, ch. 78, 5.

the Church (not the Church of Christ) has, on her own authority, made preachers of them. One order, at least, of the three in the hierarchy, is a human invention. As to the principle which Hooker here, as in many other places, lays down, viz., that the ordinance of Scripture is not violated by such inventions, we think that it is utterly erroneous. We do not stop to prove it so here, because this is not the proper place; but we shall take it up again.* Further, any one and every one knows that the Scriptural office of deacon is just as much required now as it ever was.

But if "tract of time has clear worn out those first occasions for which the deaconship was then most necessary," has tract of time in any way made it necessary to have a new order of preachers? We think not; for, while the Prelatic Church has three orders of ministers, there are many others which have but one, and such churches as the latter do the work of the Lord more effectually and successfully than the former.

Again, we ask, if the first duties for which deacons were appointed have failed, why was not the office abolished? This seems to be what we might reasonably expect. When men shall learn the art of war no more, we expect that the office of Secretary of War will be abolished; and if ever all the colonies should become independent, that the office of Colonial Secretary will share the same fate. Why then did not the office of deacon go in the same way?

But if it is absolutely necessary for the perfection of the hierarchy that an order of clergy should be invented, why not give it a new name? This would have been the best way to avoid confusion. A new order it most certainly is, for the duties of an office being changed, the office is, of necessity, changed. If the Colonial Secretary, for lack of colonies, no longer has their affairs to see after, but has given to him instead, the oversight of all things pertaining to war, he of course ceases to be Colonial Secre-

---

* Chap. ix.

tary, and becomes Secretary of War. So likewise, a deacon, if for lack of the occasions which require the services of a deacon, has given to him the duties of a preacher, ceases to be a deacon, and becomes a preacher. Why then, we ask, did the Church not give him the name of *presbyter* or *bishop*, the Scriptural names for preachers; or if the hierarchy must be made to stand by human efforts, why did he not get a new name? Was the old name not retained that God's people might not discover that something had been added to divine institutions by human authority? A politician wishing to retain one as a pensioner without that odious name, after his office has become a sinecure, a politician, we say, who would in such circumstances create a new office under the old name, would neither be thought clever nor honest : better at once to create a new one and endeavour, if possible, to find excuses for it.

But in this case, as a matter of policy, it would not do. There is, notwithstanding all that may be said about the power of the Church to set aside or add to the laws laid down by the Apostles, both among ministers and people, a very large majority which cannot be satisfied, unless there can be found something of the appearance, at least, of Divine authority for the institutions of the Church. With such people it would oftentimes be difficult to deal, if there were not some artifice at hand by which they could, in some way, have their craving satisfied. How convenient then to be able to say, well, if you are not satisfied with the Church's power to make a third order of clergy, we can show you something in the Scripture. Our third order is the deacons, so we name them; now deacons are officers of the Apostle's own appointment. It is true, that they were, at the first, appointed to attend to the poor as to their temporal necessities, but that does not prohibit their preaching; indeed we find that some of them did afterwards preach, as for example, Philip. This kind of argument, it is true, would prove that plough-boys, schoolmasters, and many others, belong to the clergy, for many of those who now are ministers, had their duties at first assigned to them in the field, the school-house, and the counting-house; and so, if the fact that Philip was a deacon, and afterwards, as an evangelist, preached, proves that deacons are preachers; even so, the fact that Peter, Andrew, and others, were fishermen, and afterwards became Apostles, likewise proves that all fishermen are Apostles; or the fact, that some are at the first plough-boys and afterwards become preachers, proves that plough-boys are preachers. But where such argument will pass current, it serves a certain purpose, just as a coin, even though made of base metal, if not detected in time, answers the ends of the counterfeiter.

The supposed Scriptural argument in favour of the third order is easily dealt with; but there is a certain kind of reasoning by those who at the outset lay down the radically unsound position that the Church has power to add to the laws given by the Apostles, where there is nothing specially prohibiting such addition; or even to set aside the positive laws of the Apostles if it seems to her that they are no longer needed, which, though easily dealt with too, is a little more plausible than the former. Here is a specimen of it from Hooker. Because the Apostles' labours were too great they appointed deacons, and he adds: "Whereupon we may rightly ground this maxim, that when the subject, wherein one man's labours of sundry kinds are employed, doth wax so great that the same men are no longer able to manage it sufficiently as before, the most natural way to help this is by dividing their charge into slips, and ordaining of under officers, as our Saviour under twelve apostles, seventy Presbyters" (a gratuitous assertion of Hooker, he has not the shadow of foundation for it excepting in his love for a false system, see page 80,) "and the apostles by his example seven deacons to be under both.(?) Neither ought it to seem less reasonable, that when the same men are sufficient, both to continue in that which they do, and also to undertake somewhat more, a combination be admitted in this case as well as division in the former. We may not therefore disallow it in the Church of Geneva, that Calvin and Beza were made both pastors and readers of divinity, being men so able to discharge both. To say they did not content themselves with their pastoral vocations, but break into that which belonged to others : to allege against them, 'He that exhorteth in exhortation,' as against us, 'He that distributeth in simplicity,' is alleged in great dislike of granting license for deacons to preach, were very hard."*

Hooker here avoids the point of his adversaries' argument, and conceals it too, with a dexterity which the prince of Jesuits might envy. The cases are not at all parallel, for both in the churches of Geneva and in all Presbyterian Churches, we ordain men to teach the people and to rule, as members of church courts, the congregation. We hold that this gives them power to teach the worshipping congregation, the Bible class, and from house to house, or in any other way or place consistent with order. If then some of them are detailed to teach those who are preparing for the office of the Ministry, do we do anything at all parallel to what the Episcopal Church does in the case of her deacons? Does she keep an order of officers for the purpose for which the Apostles set apart deacons, and does she occasionally give one of them his own peculiar duties to perform for a certain class ? If so, she does in this no more than the Presbyterian Church does in reference to her professors of theology, and no man of common sense will say that she has exceeded the Scripture warrant.

But this is not at all what she has done. She has, on the contrary, invented an inferior order of clergy, —a set of subordinate ministers, who preach and in part administer the sacraments, in addition to such duties as primitive deacons performed. But in these last duties,

---

* Laws Ecc. Pol. Book v, ch. 78, 5.

they are not distinguished from either of the other orders. They are thus no more deacons, than presbyters are deacons,—not so much deacons as are diocesans themselves; for the Apostles ordained deacons that they themselves might have all their time to preach. Diocesans have subordinate ministers (called deacons), that they may have time to attend to such things as the Church has either invented or taken upon herself to do, such as confirmations, the looking after the finances of the church, pleading for her in Parliament, getting prayers revised, when necessary, by the Privy Council, seeing that all things in the millinery department are in accordance with King Edward, and that nothing is added to or taken from the Rubric, no matter what may be added to or taken from the Word of God. When we make of our deacons, professors of theology, and when we make professors of theology inferior to pastors and teachers, then may our example be pleaded as a ground for the Episcopal diaconate; but while things remain as they are, we have no such irregularity in our Church as is to be found in the hierarchy.

Thus we have found that there is not only no Scripture in favour of the third order of the clergy in the Episcopal Church, but none which can be wrested so as to favour it, nor any which, by a mistake of interpretation, can be made to support it. We have also found that Hooker acknowledges that it is an invention of men. On this point however, as well as on others discussed, the Scripture is entirely on our side.

CHAPTER VI.

CHURCH COURTS.

WE have proved that the ministers are all of one order, and that governments, or ruling elders, are associated with them in the government of the Church. Under these circumstances, there are two, and only two, very reasonable suppositions as to the manner in which authority is to be exercised.

1. *Each congregation may be independent, and be ruled by the minister and his associate rulers as a session or governing body.*

2. *Each congregation, while governed by such a session as described above, in things of local interest, may be, along with all the other congregations, under the rulers of the whole Church, as a governing body, in things of general interest.*

These two suppositions are, of course, not all that are logically possible; but we take them as typical examples of possible ones on the two sides of the question. The supposition of a congregation's being governed by its minister alone, is not possible, when we have once proved, as we have done, that the ministers should have others associated with them in governing. Of the above suppositions, which one is in accordance with Scripture? In answer to this question, we may state, at the outset, the proposition which we are about to prove, viz.,

EACH CONGREGATION IS SUBJECT TO THE RULERS OF THE WHOLE CHURCH, ASSEMBLED AS A GOVERNING BODY OR CHURCH COURT.

The proof of the above proposition we find in the fifteenth and sixteenth chapters of the Acts. From the fourteenth chapter, we learn that Paul and Barnabas had arrived at Antioch; the fifteenth then opens with an account of the arrival of false teachers at the same place. "Certain men which came down from Judea taught the brethren, and said, Except ye be circumcised after the manner of Moses, ye cannot be saved. When therefore Paul and Barnabas had no small dissension and disputation with them, they determined that Paul and Barnabas, and certain other of them, should go up to Jerusalem, unto the apostles and elders about this question."* Here then is a congregation or number of congregations, in doubt about a matter of interest to the whole Church; yet their rulers do not undertake to decide it, but refer it to the assembly at Jerusalem, composed of the Apostles and elders, representing both the church at Jerusalem and that at Antioch, the latter sending Paul, Barnabas, and certain others. The parties appointed by the church in Antioch in due time arrive in Jerusalem, and report the matter. "The apostles and elders came together for to consider of this matter."† After much discussion Peter spoke, and next James; then, in accordance with the opinion expressed by James, and doubtless, by others also, "It pleased the apostles and elders, with the whole church, to send chosen men of their own company to Antioch with Paul and Barnabas, namely, Judas, surnamed Barsabas, and Silas, chief men among the brethren: and they wrote by them."‡ The epistle they carried and delivered to the whole multitude (*i. e.*, to the multitude of the members of the Church in Antioch), who rejoiced in the decision arrived at.

---

*Acts xv, 1, 2.   †Ibid, verse 6.   ‡Ibid xv, 22, 23.

We find moreover, that this decision was binding, not upon them alone, but also upon other churches and congregations. For it is said, after Paul and others had visited many places, that "as they went through the cities, they delivered them the decrees for to keep, that were ordained of the apostles and elders which were at Jerusalem."*

From what we have brought forward here, it appears quite clear—1. That there is such a thing as a general assembly or governing body, composed of the rulers of the whole Church or of their delegates. 2. That matters affecting the whole Church are not to be decided by any single congregation, or by the rulers of such congregation, nor yet by any number of congregations being a part of the whole Church, nor by the rulers of such congregations, but by such general assembly or governing body as is described above.

1. Objection of Independents to the doctrine of an Assembly or Synod.

Independents refer us to such passages as these: "Then pleased it the apostles and elders, with the *whole Church*, to send chosen men of their own company to Antioch;" "The apostles, and elders, and brethren send greeting." The *brethren* and the *whole Church* spoken of, they maintain, are the private members of the Church; and we say they are right so far; but we object when they infer that the fact of the whole Church and the brethren's being mentioned in this connection, makes the assembly here different from a Presbyterian synod or general assembly: for the matter was not referred to the Apostles, elders and *brethren*, but only to the Apostles and elders. It was only the Apostles and elders who met to deliberate upon the matter; the decrees were ordained by the Apostles and elders; all this is stated in so many words in the narrative. We conclude then, that the

---
*Acts xvi, 4.

brethren were present in the assembly, not as members of it, but as interested in the discussion, and that they concurred in the decision arrived at as an example to the private members at Antioch. Taking all the facts of the case, this is the only reasonable conclusion which they will admit of.

2. *Objection of the Prelatists.*

The Prelatist contends, that as James said, "Wherefore my sentence is that we trouble not them, &c. ;"* and that, as the Apostles and elders decided in accordance with what James had said, he was therefore diocesan bishop of Jerusalem.

This is a hopeless effort to save his own tottering structure, rather than an attempt to overthrow the doctrine which we have deduced from the narrative. After being informed by the inspired writer that the matter was not referred to James, but to the Apostles and elders; that it was the latter, and not the former, who considered it; that the Apostles and elders ordained the decrees; the reader can hardly be expected to believe that it was all done by James. Any one who has ever been present in an assembly, and has heard a member of it rise, after a lengthened discussion, and say, "I think that such and such should be our course, and therefore I move that we take it," will at once understand the position of James in the assembly.

We now proceed to the consideration of courts in subordination to the supreme court of the Church. The Scriptures teach that there is a

GRADATION OF CHURCH COURTS.

We have already proved that the whole Church was under one general assembly, or governing body. If we can now prove that any number of congregations in any

---

* Acts xv, 19.

part of the Church was under a local governing body, we have at once a presbytery.

We may say at the outset, that it is reasonable that there should be such a governing body as a presbytery. When once we establish the fact that there is Scripture authority for the general assembly or synod, this conclusion can scarcely be avoided. The general assembly has charge of matters of general interest; but there are often matters of interest to a number of congregations in a particular district, which are not of interest to the whole Church. Why should such matters not be disposed of by a presbytery? Again, there are many things which a small body of rulers are quite as capable of disposing of as a larger body would be; why not let a smaller number be constituted as a court for that purpose, and thus save much unnecessary trouble? We may go still farther. There are many things which can only be thoroughly understood by those in the particular districts where they may happen, or are required to be done, which makes it useless for any more than a small number to take them up.

But though, when we prove that there is authority for a synod or general assembly, we have then the essential principle of the Presbyterian church-court system, we need not stop here for want of more direct proof for the presbytery. The case of the Church at Jerusalem is sufficient for our purpose. It is called the "*church*,"* but never churches. We must either conclude that it consisted of one congregation only, or of several under one presbyterial government. Independents, in order to maintain their position, contend that the former was the case. Are they right?

In the second chapter of the Acts we have an account of the success of Peter's preaching. In the forty-first verse we are told, that "They that gladly received his word were baptized; and the same day there were added unto them about three thousand souls." At the close, it

---

* Acts viii, 1.

is said, "The Lord added to the church daily such as should be saved," showing that there was a continual increase. Not long after this, Peter again preached, and about five thousand men (probably exclusive of women and children) believed.* After this eight thousand had believed, it is said, "Believers were the more added to the Lord, multitudes both of men and women."† Again we are told, "The word of God increased, and the number of the disciples multiplied in Jerusalem greatly; and a great company of the priests were obedient to the faith."‡ All this goes to show that the increase was great indeed. Independents nevertheless contend that there was but one congregation. But we can hardly think, that they can be satisfied with their position. Let us suppose an Independent missionary to write home such an account of his success as is given in the Acts, would the brethren not be somewhat disappointed, if they should afterwards learn that he had only one congregation? Not if that one congregation were large enough, it may be answered. But a congregation is necessarily limited, first, on account of the size of places of meeting; secondly, if extremely large, one man could not rule it all. If it is said, that he may have others under him, we have Episcopacy; if it is said, that different ministers from different parts of it may meet for the purpose of jurisdiction, we have Presbyterianism. But still the advocates of Independency insist that there was only one congregation; and we now proceed to consider the passages which they quote in support of their position.

We are invited to compare this passage, "All that believed were together, and had all things common,"§ with the following, "They continuing daily with one accord in the temple, &c.;"‖ and from the comparison we are expected to learn that those mentioned before as together, found a suitable place of meeting in the temple. In reference to these passages, we may remark that the phrase

---

*Acts iv, 4. †Ibid v, 14. ‡Ibid vi, 7. §Ibid ii, 44. ‖Ibid ii, 46.

ἐπὶ τὸ αὐτὸ does not necessarily mean "*together*," *i. e., in one place*, but also *together*, as *having unity of purpose.* It is so used in this passage, "The kings of the earth stood up, and the rulers were gathered *together* against the Lord and against his Christ,"* where it is plain that the different parties did not all meet in one place. We may properly say of the whole Presbyterian Church,—of both its ministers and people,—that they are gathered (ἐπὶ τὸ αὐτὸ) *together* for any work which the Church carries on. In reference to "continuing daily in the temple," it is not said that all continued daily in the temple; for immediately connected with it, we are told that breaking of bread in different private houses was going on at the same time. But suppose that Independents could show, beyond dispute, that there was only one congregation at this time, when the number of converts was only three thousand, it would by no means follow that they still remained one, when they had increased to at least eight thousand, with a daily increase not numbered, bringing up the number to probably tens of thousands; for it is recorded that myriads believed. "Thou seest, brother, (πόσαι μυριάδες) how many *myriads* of Jews there are who believe;"† and the context, as well as what has before been related, justifies us in applying this language to the Jews of Jerusalem.

But the supposed proof of there being but one congregation, is not yet quite disposed of. We have still another passage to examine. "When they had prayed, the place was shaken where they were assembled together, and they were all filled with the Holy Ghost, and spake the word of God with boldness: and the multitude of them that believed were of one heart and of one soul;"‡ *i. e.*, the multitude of them that believed were the persons who were assembled together, and were consequently all of one congregation. We think however that it will appear very plain to any one who will take the pains to examine this passage, that

---

*Acts iv, 26. †Ibid xxi, 20. ‡Ibid iv, 31.
H

the thirty-second verse speaks of a different company from that mentioned in the thirty-first; for we cannot suppose that everyone in the multitude was filled with the Holy Ghost, and spake the Word with boldness, for then would every man, woman, and child have been a preacher. The speaking of the Word with boldness is a part of the answer to the prayer of the twenty-ninth verse; the remainder of the answer is found in the thirty-third verse, where we may well suppose that miracles were wrought in connection with preaching. Hence, in thought, the thirty-first verse is connected with the thirty-third; and the thirty-second, which introduces a new subject, is connected with the thirty-fourth, for *any* and *many* of the last mentioned verse cannot refer to the Apostles of the preceding verse, but to the multitude of the thirty-second. It was then the Apostles who were assembled together, and not the whole multitude of believers.

The argument from the fifth chapter and twelfth verse, in favour of there being only one congregation, scarcely deserves notice. It is there said, " By the hands of the apostles were many signs and wonders wrought among the people, and they were all with one accord in Solomon's porch." Therefore, all the believers could meet in one place. But is it the believers who were in Solomon's porch? We say, no; but the Apostles were. If this be denied, then it must have been the people, for either *Apostles* or *people* is the antecedent of *they*; and *people* includes not only the believers, but the inhabitants of Jerusalem, as well as those who came from a distance. Verily, Solomon's porch was a large place!

We argue, that as there were so many converts in Jerusalem, it would be impossible for them to find a place large enough for their accommodation as one congregation. But, say the Independents, they could meet in the temple. We think not. Suppose it were large enough to hold so many, can we imagine that the Jews, who worshipped in it, would give it up to a sect whom they hated and despised? Just think of some thousands of Christians assembling in the temple of those who had but lately crucified the Saviour, to commemorate His death! But still it is urged that the Apostles preached daily in the temple. We answer, not to all their followers; they preached daily in the temple rather to the unconverted Jews who went up there to worship, and to such Christians as might find it convenient to resort to the temple. This moreover exactly accords with the fact that they preached daily in many other places in Jerusalem.*

We next argue that among the converts in Jerusalem there were those who spoke Greek, viz., the Grecian Jews mentioned in the sixth chapter of the Acts; and this in itself would necessitate their having more than one congregation. It is true, that people speaking different languages might all meet together, and each company be edified in its turn; but this would involve a great loss of time, for all would have to hear much which they could not understand.

Again we inquire, how could the Apostles, who had ordinary ministers associated with them in the work, have been kept so busy preaching to one congregation, as to require the assistance asked for in the beginning of the sixth chapter of the Acts? That congregation must have had a deal of preaching!

In view of the many considerations which have been brought forward, we ask if it does not clearly appear, that the congregations of Jerusalem were numerous; and yet the whole of them is spoken of as the Church at Jerusalem, but never as the churches. Hence we infer, that they were all under one ruling body, and as this body was but a part of that which ordained the decrees before mentioned, it must have been a court inferior to it.

But we are not, in this stage of our argument, confined solely to the Church in Jerusalem. In Acts IX, and 31, it is said, "Then had the Church† rest throughout all Judea and Galilee and Samaria and was edified."

---

*Acts v, 42.   †English version, Churches.

Upon what authority do we change the text here from *churches* to *Church*? There are three old MSS., of the Bible to which all denominations bow: they are the Alexandrian, the Vatican, and the Sinaitic. These are the oldest in the possession of the Christian Church, and the three, upon the authority of which, the text of the Bible is mainly determined; and the whole three agree in giving the reading quoted above, viz., *Church*, not churches. The one next in age and authority to these, is the Codex Ephræmi, and it also agrees with them in this matter. Thus we have four of the oldest and best MSS., and we may add, several of the oldest and best translations of the Bible, all authorizing the reading which we have given; and we need hardly say, that these authorities settle the question beyond the possibility of a doubt.

"Then had the Church rest throughout all Judea and Galilee and Samaria." This one passage is quite sufficient to overthrow the Congregational view and establish our own; that the Church is one and under one governing body, in so far as the nature of things will allow of it; and also, that under the highest governing body, there are subordinate bodies such as synods or presbyteries. For the Church in Jerusalem, as well as the Church in Judea, Galilee and Samaria, would require a governing body or bodies to deal with things of local interest, and that body or those bodies would be either a synod, or presbyteries, or both, it matters not which (for the principle is the same), under a general assembly such as met at Jerusalem.

We may now sum up our argument as follows: We have an unmistakable instance of a general assembly's exercising authority over the whole Church. After having a general assembly, we saw that it was most reasonable and desirable to have subordinate courts to deal with things of local interest, and we then turned to the Scriptures on the subject. We found that a large number of congregations, as in the case of the Church in Jerusalem, as well as in that of the Church in Judea, Galilee and Samaria. were looked upon by the Apostles as one church, and must therefore have been under one and the same government; and this government must have been under the general assembly, as the churches mentioned were only a part of the whole to which the decrees of that assembly were delivered.

To the above we may add, that we do, as a matter of fact, find that a small body of rulers on several occasions dealt with things of local bearing and interest. It was such a body which referred the case from Antioch to the assembly at Jerusalem; it was such a body which set apart Paul and Barnabas to a special mission; and it was such a body which ordained Timothy, and which is mentioned by name as a presbytery.

We have now established our last proposition, viz., *The scriptures teach that there is a gradation of church courts*, and for this reason it is not necessary to continue the discussion farther; but for the satisfaction of some, it may be advisable to say a few words in reference to the session or congregational court. The same arguments which we made use of on page 111, to show the reasonableness, as well as necessity, of a presbytery may be used for the same purpose with respect to the session. Further, it appears that there must have been a session in primitive times, from the fact that there were besides the ministers, others who ruled in conjunction with them. And as every congregation must have had, at least one who preached, we infer that it must have had more than one ruler; and if it had more than one, from what we have already proved, it will follow that they must have ruled as a body or congregational court.

CHAPTER VII.

ON THE APPOINTMENT OF OFFICE-BEARERS.

THE Church, viewed Scripturally, is *one* body, of which Christ is the head; and the office-bearers, according to this view, are distinguished from the private members, only as some members of our physical bodies are distinguished from others: that is, that while office-bearers and private members have different special duties assigned to them, they have all one common interest, the highest good of the Church, and so strive together to gain that one common end. It is altogether a pagan notion which is sometimes brought forward, viz., that there are two bodies in the Church, clergy and laity, whose interests are different, and who each need safeguards against the encroachments of the other. We do not say, taking the state of things existing in some denominations, that it is not true that there are really two bodies, the clergy and the laity, each having separate interests; but the denominations which have this feature, do not possess in it a feature of the Church of Christ, but of Antichrist: and the notion which directly or indirectly endorses such a state of things is antichristian. But, says some one, impatient with our view, is it not a fact that clergy or ministers, are human beings, and therefore liable to be selfish; and are not the private members also more or less afflicted with the same weakness; why then object to safeguards against this natural propensity, which all see and deplore? Of course there should be safeguards, we reply; but here we differ: we do not think that it ever makes things any better to first endorse an antichristian principle, and then to set to work to find safeguards against its legitimate consequences; but the best way is to have principles founded upon the truth, and they will prove of themselves, our best safeguards. The proper course here, is to put before the Church, the great fact taught in the Bible, that it is one body, and has common interests, and that though the members of that body may differ as to office, yet all should work for the common good. And at the same time that we preach this great truth, let us take the Scriptural means for its realization in practical form; let the office-bearers of the body be such as the Scriptures indicate they should be, and let them be appointed in the Scriptural way, and we may rest assured, that in this way the selfishness complained of will be best met. It is not our purpose here to show who are the proper ecclesiastical officers to be appointed; we have already done this; but the question now is, *how should ecclesiastical officers be appointed and invested with office?*

The answer to this question may be given in a few words. The private members of the Church are to choose out or elect those to be ordained to office, and the elders are to ordain them. The first part of this answer we now proceed to consider under the head of

POPULAR ELECTION.

Our first argument for popular election, we get from the fact with which we set out, viz., that the Church is one body. In the natural body, every part helps to strengthen and develop every other part; if one member suffers, all the other members suffer with it, inasmuch as part of their strength must go to help the suffering member; and were it a thing possible for a new member to grow in the place of one removed, then all the other members would have to contribute towards the production of the new one. Is it then not reasonable indeed to conclude, that if that spiritual body, the Church, should need such a member as an elder or a deacon, that all the existing parts of the body should contribute their share, according to their position, in creating him?

Our next argument, we get from the fact that ecclesiastical power is not vested in the elders alone, but in the whole body of the faithful. Some maintain that it is vested in the clergy alone, as they call the ministry, and that it has been handed down from the time of the Apostles, to the present age through an uninterrupted succession of regularly ordained ministers, and without such uninterrupted spiritual descent, none can lawfully exercise ecclesiastical power. It will not however do in a matter of so great importance to take anything for granted: this apostolical succession must be proved. But we have already seen that it can not be proved, nay more, that it can be shown, beyond a doubt, that it has often been broken, and that if, out of the millions of ministers of different kinds on earth, there are a thousand who have the true succession, it is utterly impossible for any mortal to know who they are. This is as good as saying that none at all have it, for we cannot be sure that any one in particular has it. Has then lawful ecclesiastical power vanished from the earth, or if not, who has conferred it? But we may be asked, would not God in his providence preserve a thing of so much importance as apostolical succession. But the Bible does not say that it is of any importance, neither does common sense say that it is of any importance, and it is only on the supposition that God has preserved it, that it can be made to appear that it is of any importance at all. So the argument of him who would have its preservation proved on account of its importance, stated in full, amounts to this: The thing is of great importance because it has been preserved, and it has been preserved because it is of great importance.

ON THE APPOINTMENT OF OFFICE-BEARERS. 121

Let us suppose a case, which none will now think extravagant, since they know the value of apostolical succession. There is a community, say, which has no minister at all, and no means of getting one regularly ordained by the laying on of the hands of the presbytery. But in it, there are believers who have learned the way of life through such means of grace as they have had. They learn from their Bibles that they should form a church, and have ministers. Moreover, they have at least one among them qualified to be their minister. He feels too that the Lord, by his Spirit, has specially called him to that work, and the people feel that he is in every way a suitable person to be their minister: the question is, by whom shall he be invested with the ministerial character? We answer, by the whole body of the faithful. What! shall ordinary members of the Church ordain him? There is, we say, no need of ordination, when there are no office-bearers with whom he is to share ecclesiastical power. Ordination is nothing more than the recognition on the part of those members of the Church who are already elders, that one has been called in God's providence to be their fellow-elder, and that they give their willing assent to his sharing, with them, their power. Now because this recognition must take place according to God's arrangement, wherever there are elders, before one can be in lawful possession of power, we speak of the mere recognition as conferring ecclesiastical power, and we speak of those who so recognize others, as having power vested in them. This recognition confers no grace whatever, and is merely for the sake of order and harmony in the Church. Since then there were no elders in the community supposed, there would be no need of any such recognition, as there could not possibly be a want of harmony between the newly-appointed minister and those who had no existence. We see then that ecclesiastical power is vested in the whole body of believers, and hence we conclude that *all in that body should have a voice in conferring it.*

But how do we know that popular election is to be the means by which a large part of this body is to exercise its right? We shall get an answer to this question in the consideration of our third argument for the doctrine, to which we proceed.

We now come to the direct testimony of Scripture. In the beginning of the sixth chapter of the Acts we have the following, "In those days when the number of the disciples was multiplied, there arose a murmuring of the Grecians" (*i. e.*, the Jews who spoke Greek) "against the Hebrews" (Hebrew-speaking Jews) "because their widows were neglected in the daily ministration. Then the twelve called the multitude of the disciples, and said, It is not reason that we should leave the word of God and serve tables, wherefore brethren look ye out among you seven men of honest report, full of the Holy Ghost and wisdom, whom we may appoint over this business. * * * And the saying pleased the whole multitude, and they chose Stephen," &c. The fact of popular election is patent upon the face of this narrative. The passage needs no explanation. Even the Apostles, who had such great authority, never for a moment supposed that they had all to say in the appointment of ecclesiastical officers, but from the very beginning they recognized the right of the private members to elect those who should be their office-bearers.

Again it is said, "When they had ordained them elders in every church."* This passage occurs in an account of the travels of Paul and Barnabas, in which they visit many places and preach the Gospel. But what has this to do with popular election? The word translated *had ordained* should be rendered *had chosen by suffrage*, and then we see at once that it teaches popular election. This is a case similar to that in Acts twentieth and twenty-eighth, in which the translators have dealt unfairly with the original, that the Bible might not teach

---

* Acts xiv, 23.

anything contrary to their own views of Church Government; and it is to be hoped, that when we get our revised translation, we shall have both passages corrected. The original word χειροτονέω is, through χειροτόνος, from χείρ *the hand*, and τείνω *to stretch out* or *extend*. In classic Greek it means *to vote for* or *elect*. So say Liddell and Scott in these words, " *To stretch out the hand* especially for the purpose of giving one's vote in the Athenian ἐκκλησία, hence with an accusative, *to vote for, elect*." It is followed by an accusative in the passage quoted from the Acts. Dr. Robinson, who has produced a standard lexicon of the New-Testament Greek, gives the following as the meaning of the word. " *To stretch out the hand, to hold up the hand* as in voting, hence *to vote, to give one's vote* of course by holding up the hand. In the New Testament, translate, *to choose by vote, to appoint*." Alford says, and the best expositors agree with him, " χειροτ. '*cum suffragiis creassent*' Erasm.: not necessarily as the meaning of the word conventionally, —which had passed to any kind of appointment, see ch. x, 41, but by the analogy of ch. vi, 2-6. See ref., 2 Cor. The word will not bear Jerome's and Chrys's sense of *laying on* of hands, adopted by Roman Catholic expositors. Now is there any reason for departing from the usual meaning of electing by show of hands. The Apostles may have admitted by ordination those presbyters whom the churches elected."

We have now shown, ecclesiastical power being vested in the whole Church, the part which the private members have to perform in the apppointment of office-bearers, viz., *to elect* them, and this goes to show more certainly, that ecclesiastical power is vested in the whole body of believers: the two facts are mutual supports. We have now to consider the part which the elders take in the appointment of the same. To them belongs the right to ordain.

ORDINATION.

1. *What is Ordination?*

It is the last of the two acts by which the Church puts one in formal possession of ecclesiastical power. We all know that the Lord is the ultimate source of all power, and that it is the Lord who gives lawful power, even as He gives pasture to His sheep; but as He will have His sheep enter by the door, even so He has a way by which those whom he calls to be preachers and rulers must enter into the possession of that power, and in this way there are two gates, of which He has made the Church the keeper, and which she is to open whenever He calls her in His providence to do so. The first is opened in the way already described by her private members, and the second is opened by her elders by prayer and the laying on of hands, or in other words, by the ceremony of ordination.

That there is such a ceremony for this purpose alone, can be proved from Scripture. When the seven were appointed by the people, the Apostles prayed and laid their hands on them.* This was not that they might impart to them the Holy Ghost, for the people were directed to look out men "full of the Holy Ghost," and they did choose such men.† Again we are told, that the elders in Antioch, in order to obey the Holy Ghost, and set Paul and Barnabas apart to the work to which He had called them, "fasted, prayed, and laid their hands on them."‡ Nor was this to impart unto them the Holy Ghost, for they had already received Him.§ Further, Timothy is thus directed, "Neglect not the gift that is in thee, which was given thee by prophecy, with the laying on of the hands of the presbytery." That the Apostle here rather refers to the gift of office than to

---

* Acts vi, 6. † Ibid v, 5. ‡ Ibid xiii, 3.
§ See Acts ix, 17 and xi, 24.

spiritual gifts, appears from the fact that he had the latter from Paul's own hands. "Wherefore," says he to Timothy in another place, "I put thee in remembrance that thou stir up the gift of God, which is in thee by the putting on of my hands."*

2. *The necessity of Ordination*

We would have it distinctly understood at the outset, that ordination is not supposed to enable one to preach better than he could before; that it does not make one more pious than he was before; and that it confers no spiritual gifts or graces whatever. But while this is the case, it may be most necessary for other reasons. In any organized society such as the Church, in order that work may be done in the best possible manner, the greatest harmony must prevail among the workers. It would most certainly introduce discord, and tend to injure the Church very much, to force the private members to receive any one whom they thought unfit to be their teaching or ruling elder; hence the Lord Jesus has given to them the right of popular election. Just so, it would destroy that harmony which should ever be found in the Church, to compel the office-bearers to admit any one to be their fellow-labourer whom they have good grounds for rejecting. To meet this difficulty, and to preserve order in the Church, her Head has given to the Ministry the right to receive or reject any man who may desire to become an ecclesiastical office-bearer. (I need hardly say, that this right, like every other one which God has given to His people, is to be exercised only in the Lord.) Now ordination being the ceremony by which the Ministry exercises this right, it is requisite, in one word, for this end and this alone, *to get the consent of the office-bearers to one's becoming their fellow-labourer.*

---

* II Tim. i, 6.

3. To whom belongs the right to Ordain?

To the elders, we answer. We have already proved (p. 59) from the direct testimony of Scripture, that the Apostles, as ordinary officers were elders, hence in performing ordinary duties they acted as elders; and it was the Apostles who ordained the seven deacons. It was also the elders of Antioch who ordained Paul and Barnabas for the special work to which the Holy Ghost had called them, and Timothy was ordained by the laying on of the hands of the presbytery, or elders constituted as a church court. We need hardly prove this here, as we have already shown that there are no officers in the Church superior to elders, and none claim that deacons have the right to ordain. We see moreover that ordination is not performed by one man, but by a number; this also, we need hardly state, as we have already shown that the elders do not perform any act of government as individuals, but as members of church courts.

But it is more satisfactory to many to dwell upon every point. We do not then find that the Apostles ever ordained singly, but always as a presbytery. Nor can it be shown that any one alone ever ordained. It is claimed that Titus did, but as he was a subordinate to the Apostles, and as an Apostle tells him to ordain* elders in accordance with his appointment, we take it that Paul tells him to call upon the people to elect them, and afterwards for him to have them ordained by a presbytery. This was what Paul did himself, and we cannot suppose that he directed his evangelist to act in a different way.

CONCLUSION.

We have now concluded our remarks upon this subject, from which it appears that ecclesiastical power, being vest-

---

* Not to lay hands alone upon men, but to appoint men to the eldership, is the meaning of the word in the original.

ed in the whole Church, is conferred by the whole Church; that church officers are regularly invested with authority, by being first elected by the private members, and afterwards ordained, by prayer and the laying on of hands, by the elders; and to this there is but one exception, viz., when the whole Church is made up of private members: then election alone is sufficient to invest an officer with uthority.

CHAPTER VIII.

THE HEADSHIP OF CHRIST.

THE QUESTION STATED.

WE have already, among other things, established the fact that ecclesiastical power is vested in the Church of Christ as composed of both private members and office-bearers. We have now to inquire from whom that power is directly derived? By this inquiry, we do not mean to imply that there is any difference of opinion as to the final source of all lawful power both in Church and State; all acknowledge that God Himself is that source. Nor is there any difference of opinion as to the power of Christ; all admit, that as the second person of the Trinity, He is equal to the Father, and has the same power; and further, that as Mediator, in which office He has assumed and holds a subordinate position, He has committed unto Him all power in heaven and in earth,* and that He is therefore, "the Prince of the kings of the earth,"† as well as the source of all lawful power exercised in the Church. Still further, all agree that there are rulers under Christ to administer His laws. The only question about which there is

---

* Matth. xxviii. 18.   † Rev. i, 5.

any difference is this, *has the Church any head over her under Christ?* Says the Papist, the pope is her head; the Episcopalian cries, the head of the State is her head; while we maintain that Christ is her head, and Christ alone—that Christ is her head in every sense.

THE POPE OF ROME IS NOT THE HEAD OF THE CHURCH.

We have already found that the rulers are elders, and besides these, that there are no others mentioned in Scripture, who have not ceased to exist as rulers in the Church, and these facts effectually shut out all other rulers whatsoever, whether ecclesiastical or civil, and virtually overthrow the Papal and Episcopal systems. But that building, the foundation of which is destroyed, and which, to the near observer, is seen to be a hopeless ruin, may still, while the stones of the upper parts remain untouched, appear to one farther off, a substantial structure; so Prelacy, even while its foundations are sapped, may appear, to those who do not think, to remain in a great measure as good as ever. For the sake then of those who do not look closely at its pitiable condition, we proceed to level the last remnant of it. In this renewal of the attack upon the fallen fabric, we shall begin with the gigantic topstone of the complete Prelatic building, viz., the pope.

Christ might have appointed one man over all His ministers if He, in His wisdom, had seen fit; but we maintain that He has not done so, because we cannot find any account of such a thing. The Papist however contends that He has made such an appointment in the person of the pope, who is His vicar upon earth. If He has, we ask for proof. This is surely a just demand. Lo, here it is! To Peter was given power to uphold the Church on earth, and to open heaven for his fellow man, or to shut it against him. Peter was the first bishop of Rome, and the pope is consequently his successor and the inheritor of his power. Where, we ask again, is the proof of Peter's superiority? The following passage, says the Papist, is the proof. "I say also unto thee, that thou art Peter (Πέτρος) and upon this rock (πέτρᾳ) I will build my church; and the gates of hell shall not prevail against it. And I will give unto thee the keys of the kingdom of heaven; and whatsoever thou shalt bind on earth shall be bound in heaven; and whatsoever thou shalt loose on earth shall be loosed in heaven."* A single passage, but still abundantly sufficient, if the Papist's interpretation of it will stand the test.

To establish a doctrine on a single passage of Scripture, we hold that the following condition must not be violated: the passage must not admit of more than the one interpretation upon which the doctrine is founded; to give it another, would be to do part or all of three things:—1, to violate grammatical usage; 2, to outrage common sense; and 3, to establish a doctrine contrary to the general tenour of Scripture. If, to any passage then on which it is sought to found a doctrine, another interpretation different from that on which such a doctrine is founded can be given, without doing any of the three things above mentioned, that passage is insufficient for the purpose for which it is sought to be used. For it is plain, that if we could give more than one interpretation of a passage, we could not be sure which was the right one, and consequently we could not be sure of the soundness of our doctrine. It is also plain, that any interpretation of a passage which involves the doing of any one of the three things above-mentioned, is not the correct one.

In reference to the passage before us, can no meaning but the Papist's be taken from it without doing violence to grammatical usage or common sense, or without establishing a doctrine contrary to the tenour of Scripture? We think it is easily interpreted in a quite different way without committing any of the above-mentioned mistakes. The Papist finds his consolation in the word

---

* Matth. xvi, 18, 19.

THE HEADSHIP OF CHRIST.   131

rock. "Thou art Peter (literally a rock), and upon this rock I will build my Church," *i. e.*, upon Peter I will build my Church. As to Christ, using two words the same in meaning and almost the same in form, (the first is Petros masculine gender, the second is petra fem.), while He applies them to totally different things, we may remark, that He did what was customary and well understood among the people whom He taught. Jeremiah does something of the same nature. Says this Prophet, "What seest thou? and I said I see a rod of an almond tree, (שָׁקֵד shakād), then said the Lord to me, thou hast well seen for I will hasten (שֹׁקֵד shokād) my word to perform it."* The names it was customary to give to persons, afforded frequent opportunities for such a paronomasia. Take *e. g.*, the words of Esau to his father on the occasion of his losing the blessing, "Is he not rightly named Jacob, for he hath *supplanted* me these two times."† The ordinary English reader here, as in the passage from Jeremiah, misses the point of the remark, because the resemblance between the words used is lost in the English. In Gen. xxv. 26, it will be seen why the name *Jacob* was given; he took his brother by the heel, and this name was bestowed, which interpreted is, *he will take hold of the heel*. To return to the former passage, Esau says, "Is he not rightly named, *He-will-take-hold-of-the-heel*, for he hath taken hold of my heel" (*i. e.*, tripped me up, supplanted me) "these two times." Numerous examples of this kind of play upon words may be found in the Scripture. If the reader is surprised at this, let him remember, that what is in our language undignified, was not at all so, but quite proper and even elegant, in the oriental languages. In speaking to Peter, Christ, we say, made use of a paronomasia, which custom had made very familiar to the people to whom He spoke. Now the very fact, that in such a play upon words, one is made slightly different

---

* Jer. i, 11, 12.   † Gen. xxvii, 36.

from the other, shows clearly that the teacher intends, that one shall not be mistaken for the other; hence when Christ says, ἐπὶ ταύτῃ τῃ πέτρᾳ, *upon this rock*, he uses the word πέτρᾳ and makes it emphatic by the words ταύτῃ τῃ (*this the*) on purpose to distinguish it from Πέτρος. If πέτρᾳ is not the same thing as Πέτρος, it may be asked, what does it signify? It is the truth (ἡ ἀλήθεια) agreeing in gender with πέτρᾳ, announced by Peter in the sixteenth verse, "*Christ the Son of the living God.*" This accords exactly with the grammatical structure of the passage, and also with the teaching of the Bible in every other place. Jesus had asked the disciples, "Who do men say that I, the Son of Man, am?" they answered, "Some say that thou art John the Baptist, some Elias, and others Jeremias or one of the prophets." Now any of these might have been a christ, that is, one anointed for a special office; but none of them could do the work which Christ came to do. No mere man, however holy, could be accepted as a substitute to die for his fellow-men—no, not the highest created being, for all belong to God, and have no right to give their lives away. Besides, the life of one man, if it could be accepted, could only save one. The substitute must then be one who has power to lay down his life and power to take it again, and be possessed of a life valuable enough to redeem all, he must then be God; hence it was not enough to say "thou art *a christ*," but when it was said "Thou art *Christ, the Son of the living God,*" Christ was declared to be God equal with the Father; the truth was announced which makes the sacrifice of Christ efficacious, and which lies at the foundation of a blood-washed Church, against which, so founded, the gates of hell cannot prevail.

As to the power of the keys, whatever it may amount to, we remark first, that there was no power conferred upon Peter which was not conferred on the other Apostles. It will at once be admitted by all, that the power of the keys is contained in these words, "Whatsoever thou shalt bind on earth, shall be bound in heaven; and whatsoever thou shalt loose on earth, shall be loosed in heaven." Well, to all the Apostles it was said, "Whatsoever ye shall bind on earth, shall be bound in heaven; and whatsoever ye shall loose on earth, shall be loosed in heaven."* What becomes of Peter's supremacy? We remark secondly, that the power here conferred is that which the lawfully appointed rulers in Christ's Church have, when they faithfully administer the laws which He has given for the government of the Church. And of course what is done in conformity with these laws, will be ratified in heaven; therefore it is promised, "Whatsoever ye shall bind on earth, shall be bound in heaven," &c.

Nor is this a mere conjecture, for we find that the Apostles never exercised any such power as the Papist claims for Peter; nor did any of them ever acknowledge the authority of Peter to be greater than his own; nor did Peter ever claim any such power. It is reasonable too to limit their power by the laws which Christ gave, as no officer under the king can lawfully do more than the laws of that king warrant him in doing. Though discretionary powers are sometimes given, yet this is only done in cases of emergency, and it is done too for a reason which cannot hold in the case of Christ. The earthly king gives discretionary power, because he does not know, and cannot know the circumstances under which that power will require to be exercised; but Christ knows all things, and has no need of any to exercise such power for Him.

We have now given an interpretation of this passage entirely different from that of the Papist. We do not say that we are right, but we can say this, that our interpretation, so far from doing violence to grammatical construction, is in perfect accordance with the same. It is also perfectly reasonable, and further, consists with the whole tenour of Scripture on the subject. We therefore

---

* Matth. xviii, 18.

conclude, that this single passage is at least insufficient for the purpose of the Papist.

But we have not yet finished. We shall now test the interpretation of our opponent. He builds a most important doctrine upon the passage, viz., that supreme power in the Church was given to Peter, in virtue of which the dispensation of all the blessings purchased by Christ was placed in Peter's hands, so that he could give or withhold them, according as he judged it best; (thus he had power to open and shut the kingdom of heaven); and that the pope, being the lawful heir of Peter, has the same power; so that all, who do not receive the blessings of salvation from the pope, cannot receive them at all, and consequently are lost. Now if this doctrine is true, it is just as important that men should know it, as it is that they should know of the work of salvation done by Christ. But the latter is clearly taught. Christ crucified and risen is the Alpha and Omega of Scripture. How numerous are the invitations to come to Him. How many assurances are given that all sin may be washed away by His blood. If there be but one channel through which these blessings flow, it should be as clearly pointed out as the blessings themselves. We must then call upon the Papist to show us the pope's supremacy set forth in unmistakable language, and we again bring him to the Word of God for this purpose.

Four different inspired authors, Matthew, Mark, Luke, and John, have written the life of Christ. We have examined a passage in the narrative of the first, that the Papist pretends, supports a doctrine which, if true, is one of the most important ever proclaimed to man. The passage from which such a doctrine can be legitimately drawn, must be a very important one. Did the other three of Christ's biographers think it of so much account? Certainly not, for they all omit it. Mark, it is supposed by some, abridged from Matthew. And early tradition, a thing of great moment in the Church of Rome, informs us that he was associated with Peter himself as his secretary;

and notwithstanding all this (if it be true), he, with the Gospel of Matthew before him, and with the superintendence of Peter who could surely look after his own supremacy, if he possessed such a thing, passed by the famous passage. He speaks of the question asked by the Saviour, "Who do men say that I am;"* he gives the opinions of the people as expressed by the disciples; he gives the question put to Peter, and Peter's opinion; but he makes no account of the words so dear to the Papist. Luke† also notices the same things of which Mark speaks, and omits the very things which Mark omits, viz., the words spoken to Peter about the keys, and the opening and shutting of the kingdom of heaven. John also, like the others, makes no mention of any extraordinary power conferred upon Peter. Now, whatever may have been the peculiar circumstances of these men which would determine them to record anything in favour of Peter, or to omit the same, we know that they were all guided by the Spirit, and nothing deemed of importance by Him, would have failed to appear in their narratives. The natural inference is, that the passage cannot teach the doctrine of the Papist.

Again, if Peter had the power ascribed to him, we may reasonably look for its exercise at the very beginning of, and all along in the history of the establishment of the Christian Church. For as Bungener remarks, "Here, in fact, we have not to do with an idea of which, as of some others, it may be said, that Jesus Christ has been content to leave it to His Church as it were in the germ, committing the care of its development to human intelligence, aided by the Holy Ghost. But we have to do with a fact, and a fact which might and ought, if the Apostles had admitted it, to have distinctly developed itself from the very earliest days of the Church, and of which we are entitled to desire to have traces immediately after the Saviour's death."‡ Following up, as we have already

---

* Mark viii, 27.   † Luke ix, 18.
‡ Hist. C. Trent, p. 383, 2nd Ed., T. Constable, Edin.

done in the case of the writers of the Gospels, Bungener's train of thought, we take the history of the Christian Church from its commencement, and search, if haply we may find the supremacy of Peter. In the Acts of the Apostles, we get the commencement of Church history under the New Dispensation. In the very first chapter, Peter is brought before us. We find him forward to speak, it is true, (and so he was before the words in Matthew were spoken to him), but he does not take upon himself to do anything, tending to show that he had more power than any of the rest of the Apostles. When an Apostle was to be appointed in the room of Judas, we might expect the pope, if such were then in existence, to make the appointment. Peter however put on no popish airs. He did not send the pallium to Matthias, but the hundred and twenty disciples appointed two, and the lot decided which of these should be taken. In the second chapter, those convicted of sin by the preaching of Peter, who stood up with the *eleven*, ask the *Apostles*, "What must we do?" And it is said in the forty-second verse, "They continued steadfastly in the *apostles'* doctrine." Peter cured the lame man, but the other Apostles also wrought miracles. When the seven deacons were appointed, a most important transaction, nothing less than the introduction of a new order of office-bearers into the Church, Peter's name is not mentioned in connection with it. The Apostles direct the disciples to look them out, and the twelve lay their hands upon them, and set them apart to their office. When Peter admitted Gentiles into the Church, they that were of the circumcision, both Apostles and brethren, contended with him; but Peter, so far from answering, I am the primate infallible (whether an Œcumenical Council thinks so or not), and you have no right to question what I do, gave them a satisfactory explanation, condescending to go into all the particulars.

We now come to the writings of another Apostle—to those of Paul. None of the inspired writers, with the exception of Moses, fills so large a space in the Bible as Paul; no part of the Bible is of more importance to the Christian Church than his epistles; no one was more earnest in the work of his Master, or more anxious that sinners should know the way of life, than he; yet in all his writings he does not give one hint that Christ had appointed an Apostle as the head of the Church; nor does he for a moment suppose, that salvation, purchased by Christ, comes to man through any such channel. Why should he, who was ever careful to see that he did not "run in vain," leave that matter in the dark which must be known and acted upon by all who would be saved, if the doctrine of the Papist be true, when he knew the consequences: why should he commit such an act of perfidy against those whose spiritual oversight was committed to him? We cannot believe that he did so; there could not have been any such facts to be made known as the Papist would have us believe.

But not only did Paul not tell others of Peter's supremacy, he did not acknowledge it himself. In one of his epistles he says, "When Peter was come to Antioch, I withstood him to the face, because he was to be blamed,"* and further on in the same epistle he says, "When I saw that they" (Peter and others) "walked not uprightly, according to the truth of the gospel, I said unto Peter before them all, If thou, being a Jew, livest after the manner of Gentiles, and not as do the Jews, why compellest thou the Gentiles to live as do the Jews:" a strange thing, indeed, to say to Peter, if he had the power of binding and loosing whatever he pleased; strange too that Paul, if Peter were supreme, should show him, that he must not compel the Gentiles to be circumcised. What a mild pope (?) Peter must have been! He not only suffered Paul to escape excommunication, but also left him without warning as to the risk which he ran. Besides, he took Paul's advice, and no doubt thanked

---

* Gal. ii, 11.

him for it, for he afterwards calls him his "beloved brother."*

To crown all this, Peter himself did not claim any power over his fellows, and his modesty is in striking contrast to the arrogant assumptions of popes and their subordinates. "The elders which are among you I exhort who am also an elder," or who am a fellow-elder. Peter claims nothing more than the other Apostles possessed, and, as an ordinary officer, no authority beyond that of a presbyter.

So much for the support which the Papist's doctrine has from the general tenour of Scripture. We may say now, that the context, if he had cared to examine it, would have shown him that the Church was not said by Christ to be built upon Peter. In the twenty-third verse, after Peter had rebuked the Lord, the Lord says to him, "Get thee behind me, Satan, for thou art an offence unto me." If Peter, in the one verse, is the rock on which the Church is built, much rather is he, in the other, Satan, for in the former, it can at best only be inferred that *this rock* means Peter, from the resemblance between the words πέτρᾳ and Πέτρος, but here the Lord directly addresses him as Satan; the Church must then, if built upon Peter, be built upon Satan—upon an offence (σκάνδαλον) a stumbling-block. We do not mean to say, that the passage teaches that Peter is Satan; but that interpretation, which requires us to understand him to be the foundation of the Church, would, if consistent, require us still more emphatically to believe him to be Satan.

To sum up: the passage considered can be easily interpreted in a way entirely different from that in which the Papist interprets it, without departing from grammatical usage, but by keeping strictly in accordance with it; without doing violence to human reason, but by taking the most rational course; and without establishing anything contrary to the general tenour of Scripture, but by

---

* II. Peter iii, 15.

bringing everything into perfect harmony with the same. On the other hand, the interpretation of the Papist does violence to grammatical usage, by confounding a noun of the masculine gender with one of the feminine, and it does violence also to the idiom of the oriental languages, by confounding the two different words on which the paronomasia is founded: the very purpose for which they are used requiring them to be kept separate. It also establishes a doctrine which does violence to the very nature which God has given us, and a doctrine entirely out of harmony with the whole tenour of Scripture. We can then be just as certain that the Papist is mistaken, as if a messenger from heaven should come and declare it with a voice of thunder.

There is then no possibility of establishing the supremacy of Peter on anything which the Bible contains; on the contrary it can be clearly shown, that he had no such power, and here the first stage in the Papist's argument entirely breaks down. But suppose it had stood the test, how could he establish the second, viz., that the pope is the lawful heir or successor of Peter.

According to tradition, that apostle died A.D. 66; when was he bishop of Rome? Let us hear Bungener on this matter. He says, "The book of Acts shows him to have been at Jerusalem, at Cæsarea, at Antioch, until the year 51 or 52. Thus already we have but fourteen or fifteen years left over. Were these fourteen or fifteen years passed in Rome? In the year 57 or 58, St. Paul writes the epistle to the Romans, the longest of his epistles, and not a remembrance, not an allusion, not a word is there for the alleged founder and head of the church to which he writes; nay more, he who at the close of his letters salutes ordinarily no more than five or six persons, and often not so many, on this occasion salutes twenty-seven, and Peter is not among them. In the year 62 or 63 he writes from Rome to the churches of Philippi, Ephesus, and Colosse; he gives them a multiplicity of details about what he has seen and heard, yet not a word about Peter. In 66, the very year of his death, again he writes from Rome to Timothy. He tells him his position, his isolation, his sufferings: 'All men forsook me,' says he. * * * Where then was Peter?"* It is clear that he could not have been Bishop of Rome.

Is it any wonder then that Rome hates the Bible, and virtually makes it a sealed book. It has nothing at all to support her pretensions, but on the contrary everywhere condemns them, and points out him who is her head, by unmistakable delineations, as Antichrist, the man of sin, and son of perdition. Nor can she find support for her pretensions in any quarter; history condemns her from first to last, and shows plainly that the pope has reached his position by ambition, intrigue, and corruption. Her own conduct condemns her: it points her out as ambitious and deceitful, blood-thirsty and murderous; and her impudence, in claiming to be the Church of the meek and lowly Jesus, is unsurpassed in the annals of the human race.

THE CIVIL MAGISTRATE AS SUCH, NO MATTER HOW HIGH HIS AUTHORITY MAY BE IN CIVIL AFFAIRS, HAS NO AUTHORITY WHATEVER IN THE CHURCH, MUCH LESS IS HE THE HEAD THEREOF.

Church and State entirely separate organizations.

The different doctrines held upon the relation between Church and State may be summed up in the following statements:—

1. Church and State are identical.
2. The Church is part of the machinery of the State, and is consequently under State control.
3. The State is part of the machinery of the Church, and consequently is subject to ecclesiastical authority.
4. Church and State are perfectly distinct and independent organizations.

---

* Hist. C. Trent, p. 389; 2nd ed. T. Const., Edin.

It may be said, that these four propositions include all that it is possible to teach in reference to the relations between Church and State. Such an assertion may at first appear unwarrantable, but still, we think, all doctrines on the subject, and all possible doctrines on it, must arrange themselves under one or other of these four: besides, only one of the four can possibly be true. To ascertain the truth then, we have only to discover in which proposition it is embodied, and immediately the remaining three must be given up as false.

We all know what an organized society is; it is a body of men associated together for the gaining of some object or objects, which they could not gain at all, or which they could not so well gain as individuals. Such organizations with us are numerous: we have them for the publishing of papers, for the manufacture of articles of commerce, for the sale of such articles, for the building of railways, for the opening up of new country, and for many other things. Such societies as the above are usually called companies. Again, we have organizations for the extension of Christ's kingdom in the heathen world, for the promotion of the temperance cause, for the relief of the poor, and for other things of a like nature. Such organizations as the latter are usually called societies. But whether called societies or companies, the principle underlying them all is the same, viz., the organization is for the purpose of gaining ends which could not be gained at all, or could not be so well gained by individuals. Now the Church is just a body of men organized for the gaining of certain ends, and the State is also a body of men organized for the gaining of certain ends. Are Church and State but two names for the same society, or are they names of societies as distinct as a missionary society and a railway company?

They are not separate and distinct, says one, but being composed of the same individuals, and [having the same great end to gain, we can but regard their names, Church and State, as names applied to one great society under different aspects.* All this is very plausible, but might as much not be said of any two societies whatever? We can easily suppose a temperance society and a railway company to be composed of the same individuals, and to have the same great end in view, viz., the good of man; and yet in common language, we should pronounce them entirely separate and distinct organizations. It must appear to any thinking mind, that the distinguishing characteristics of a society are not to be found in the individuals composing it, for they were individuals before; but in the laws by which they bind themselves together, the officers which they appoint to preside over their affairs, and in the specific ends for which they strive,—in a word, in those things which *make* a society of individuals. From this it follows, that societies are distinguished the one from the other, not by the cut of the hair, the colour of the face, nor by the length of the garments of the individuals who compose them; but by their officers, laws, and the specific ends which they seek to compass.

Let us suppose a railway company to be made up of eight gentlemen, whom we shall call A, B, C, D, E, F, G, and H. They have laws for their guidance, officers to conduct their affairs, and to see that the laws are carried out; and the specific ends which they, as a company, seek, are the building and working of a certain railway. A is president; B, vice-president; C, secretary; and D, treasurer: these have been chosen to their respective offices, because the members of the company discerned in them the necessary qualifications to enable them to discharge their duties in the different places allotted to them. Let us again suppose the same individuals associated as a missionary society. New laws are now made, and new officers appointed. H is thought to be the best qualified for the office of president in this new society, and consequently he is appointed; for similar reasons, G, F, and

---

* See Hooker Ec. Pol.

E are appointed vice-president, secretary, and treasurer, respectively. The end, which this new society proposes for itself, is the spread of the Gospel in some particular field chosen because it seems, to those interested in the matter and best able to judge, to be that field where most good can be done by the society.

Both societies set to work, the one, to educate the inhabitants of an island in the South Seas, the other, to build a railway in Canada. The railway company holds a meeting, and F, more zealous in the missionary than the railway cause, proposes that a grant of money be made for the preaching of the Gospel along the line of railway; it is at once refused. "What!" says the zealous F, "are you such heathens as to refuse the Gospel to those who work on your railway?" Says the president: "I am paid to give my attention to the railway; our constitution binds us to build a railway; we raised our money for the avowed purpose of building a railway; and we would commit a great sin, if we appropriated our funds to any other purpose." "But have we not," says F, "a missionary society, and can we not appropriate some of its funds for the purpose?" A, the president, replies, "I am not head of the missionary society but of the railway company, and have nothing to say in the matter." H, president of the missionary society, endorses the above, and adds, "it will be time enough to consider missionary work when we meet as a missionary society; further, we have committed ourselves to an island in the South Seas, and have raised money for the evangelization of the inhabitants of that island, and president A has no more right or power to call us away from that field, than we have to force him to abandon his Canadian railway, in order to build one in our far off island." "But," replies the incorrigible F, "may not the railway company at least suggest to the missionary society that it could undertake work along the line of railway." H answers, "it might suggest such a thing if it choose to go beyond its own work, but then there is no use in such a suggestion, for in the course of time every member and officer of this company will meet as a missionary society, and then they may make use of any knowledge of the world which they possess, no matter how they have obtained it, and if it be deemed desirable after all suggestions are considered, to change the field of labour, or to undertake another, the missionary society will make the alterations, and undertake the new work." "What difference does this way of doing the work make?" inquires F. "All the difference in the world," answers H. "As a missionary society we meet under a constitution fitted to guide us, and different altogether from the railway company's constitution. As a missionary society we have officers to direct our affairs, who may reasonably be supposed to know most about them; we then hear suggestions from Mr. A, not as president of a railway company, but as a private member of a missionary society; we thus allow the railway company to attend exclusively to railways, and the missionary society to attend exclusively to missions, and who will venture to say, that in this way, better railways will not be built and also more missionary work done? Further, money raised for building a railway is only honestly applied when applied to that purpose, and the same with respect to that raised for missionary purposes."

"But," says F, "by thus restricting the railway company to its own work, do you not make it the whole duty of some men at least to build railways?" "No," answers H, "we make it the sole duty of the company as a company, but not the only duty of the individuals composing that company. As we have already seen, we do not forbid their becoming members of other societies, nor yet their doing, as individuals, as much good as they please." "But," F again asks, "do you not then make the railway company, as a company, ignore religion altogether?" H replies, "not at all. It is you, Mr. F, that would teach us to ignore religion. Religion teaches us to keep faith with our neighbours, and if we raise money to build a railway, to do that work with it; religion teaches us to obey those rules which enable men to work together as societies, not to break them; religion teaches an officer appointed to oversee a particular work, to give his special attention to that work alone, not to other works. If then it is right to build a railway, we may look to God for a blessing on our work, and looking to God is the foundation principle of religion."

In the above illustration, we have supposed the railway company and missionary society to be composed of the same individuals, and yet it appears that the societies are perfectly distinct; hence Church and State may be composed of the same individuals and yet be perfectly distinct societies. This supposition puts the case in the most favourable light for our opponents. If we suppose the railway company to be made up of A, B, C, D, E, F, G, H, I, J, and K, and the missionary society of only A, B, C, and D, then all of our objections would hold against the confounding of the one with the other, besides many additional objections. Now it is a fact, that while the Church might be represented by A, B, and C, it would require A, B, and C, and many more to make the State, so we may conclude after the manner of Euclid; if two societies composed of the same individuals may be perfectly distinct as societies, with greater reason may two societies, the one embracing only a part of the individuals in the other, be regarded as distinct. Therefore if the supposed railway company and missionary society can be shown to be distinct, we may with greater reason be able to show that Church and State are distinct.

If then we can show,

1. That the specific ends which Church and State seek to gain are distinct;
2. That they have different constitutions and laws;
3. That their officers are different and require different qualifications;

we prove conclusively that the two societies are perfectly distinct. I we can add to this, that evil results have always followed the confounding of the two societies, not only in the retarding of their respective works, but also in the positive injury of their members, we prove again, not only that they are distinct, but that he, who confounds them, commits a great sin.

1. *Church and State have each its own specific ends to gain, and these ends are different.*

It is true, one may say, that they have the same end in view, viz., the good of man ; but then all societies have in view the good or supposed good of man. The good of man may be divided into different departments, and what we mean is, that Church and State work in different parts of this great field, the good of man. The State seeks man's temporal good in a certain way, and the Church seeks both his eternal and temporal good, but the latter not in the way in which the State seeks it, but in such a manner as not in any way to infringe upon the prerogatives of the State. We do not say, while we thus point out the different spheres of the two great organizations of men, that either is wholly to lose sight of the whole good of man, but with the understanding that each keeps it in view, we have set down what we think each should contribute to its accomplishment. It may perhaps be asked in surprise, ought not the State to seek man's eternal good too? We reply by asking, what need is there for men associated together as a State, to undertake that which they could do much better if associated as a Church; why not organize themselves in the best form for so important a work? If already organized as a Church, so much the stronger reason is there why they should as a State leave such matters alone. Then, says another, you would have the State pay no regard to man's eternal interests at all; you would have it make laws, and carry them out, no matter how much they warred against man's eternal interests. I would have no such thing. Man's greatest temporal good is not inconsistent with his eternal good; on the contrary when his greatest temporal good is gained, then is he in the most favourable state as to his eternal good; and thus no State, while performing its duty by looking after man's temporal good, can do anything against his eternal interests; and hence while the State seeks to perform its own work, it must ever guard against injuring man's spiritual interests, for not only would this in itself be a grievous wrong, but by committing it, man would be injured in temporal things. But be it remembered, that it is one thing to guard against injuring one as to his eternal interests, and another thing to seek such interests.

But to show more clearly the difference between Church and State in this matter, let us take, for example, their treatment of their members with respect to the laws which are common to both. Both forbid stealing, but the treatment of the thief first by the one and next by the other, differ precisely as their respective ends above-mentioned differ. The State shuts the thief up in prison for a number of months or years, after which he is free to go forth and enjoy all the privileges of a citizen again. For what is he imprisoned, for temporal or for eternal good? Not for eternal good, or we should naturally expect the State to begin with that which puts eternal interests in peril. But is such the case? No. Stealing is a sin, and as such, soul-polluting. But sin consists in motives as well as in outward acts, or in other words, no outward act, apart from the motive which gave it birth, is a sin. As far as eternal interests are concerned then, the thief is the greatest loser—his soul is injured, only the property of another is injured. Is it then for the cure of the thief's soul that he is incarcerated? Not at all, for even though he should come forth from his prison declaring his determination to steal again, yet the State will not on that account prolong his imprisonment a day beyond the period of his sentence, nor deprive him of a single privilege on account of his soul's remaining unchanged. It shuts him up simply that property may be safe both from him and from others who may be deterred from committing a similar crime for fear of the punishment. It may be that the individual who lost his property was spiritually benefited or spiritually injured by the loss, yet the State inquires not as to that in meting out punishment to the thief, it looks simply at the good of society as far as property is concerned.

If this does not make our case plain enough, let us take a sin in which the temporal interests of society are not concerned. Fornication is a great sin—it is not too much to say that it is a highway to hell—and yet the State does not punish it at all. It is the same with lying: unless some temporal interest is involved, what action does the State take against it? and yet all liars shall have their part in the lake which burns with fire and brimstone.

Further, we all rebel against any interference of the State with us for doing those things which may greatly peril our eternal happiness, if they do not clash with the temporal interests of society. I may cherish feelings of hatred or revenge to my soul's great injury, but what would I say, and what would the community say, if, because I made it known, I should be arrested, condemned, and sent to the penitentiary? Nevertheless it may peril my eternal interests, and also the eternal interests of others, a thousand times more than if I were to steal.

On the other hand, how does the Church regard the thief? It just takes up the case where the State stops. Its great concern is the eternal interest of the thief himself. It lays no corporal punishment upon him for his crime, but it exhorts him to seek a change of mind, and is never satisfied until he does get this changed mind. It lays before him the awful consequences of his sin to himself, as well as the wrong it may do his fellow-men, in view both of this world and the world to come, and exhorts him to repent and prepare for eternity.

And while contrasting the Church with the State, it is good to observe how well calculated the organization of each is for its peculiar work. That man, whose whole soul would rebel against the use of force to make him look after the interests of his soul, and who, instead of being improved by such force, would be made much worse, may at once listen to persuasion, or if he do not, no evil principle will, by it, be strengthened. Now the Church has the soul's interests to look after, and persuasion is one of the fundamental principles of her constitution. Again, the desperate villain may be intent upon injuring the lives and property of others, and it would be very unwise to bring nothing to bear upon him except persuasion, for though in the end it might succeed, in the meantime much mischief may be done. For the sake then of the temporal interests of society, force must be used. But who shall employ force? The State most certainly, for it is one of the fundamental principles of its constitution; and at the same time, it is just for the performance of the State's duty, that the force is to be used, viz., to protect the temporal interests of society.

But it may be asked, cannot the State use persuasion too. Such a question could only be asked by those who fail to distinguish between an organized society and an individual. A society is made up of individuals, acting under a particular constitution and laws, for given ends. Without such constitution and laws there would be no society. Now it is just because societies have particular constitutions and laws that we give names to them; and if they should alter the fundamental principles of their constitutions, they would become different societies, and we should give them different names. Force then, being a fundamental principle of the State's constitution, and persuasion not being one, if it should either give up force or accept persuasion, it would cease to be the State, and become either a Church or an amalgamation of Church and State, the very thing which we are contending against.

Why not amalgamate them? Just because the proper cultivation of the nature of man requires the two, and requires that they should be separate, lest persuasion only should be used where force is required, or lest force should be used where persuasion only is required. Suppose two men each having one particular weapon, and each his own particular work to do with it. While things remained so, no mistakes could be made, either with respect to the work or to the use of the weapon wherewith to perform it. But suppose these two men converted into one, and the work of both given him to do with the weapons of both, then he may often use the wrong weapon instead of the right one. So also is it with Church and State.

Again it may be asked, does not the Church seek the temporal welfare of men; and if so, does she not encroach upon the prerogatives of the State. We reply, she may look after certain temporal interests, or rather after temporal interests in a certain way, without infringing upon the prerogatives of the State: for the latter does not undertake to advance the temporal interests of its subjects in every possible way. It may, for example, imprison for a time, the thief, but it is not bound to look after the temporal interests of that thief, except in the same way that it looks after those of other men; it is not bound to furnish him with employment when he comes out of prison, and yet for the want of employment he may be sorely tempted to steal again. The Church however may look after his temporal good in this way, so as to better insure his eternal good. But it does not, in such a case, take to itself any of the prerogatives of the State; neither would the State, in doing the same work, if thereby it thought crime would be lessened, be encroaching upon the prerogatives of the Church. The fact is that the seeking of temporal good in this way is common ground for any society or individual that may be in a position to undertake it. It is different altogether where laws must be enforced, depriving us of religious privileges or natural rights.

But it may still be objected, if the State looks only to temporal ends, and administers laws only for the gaining of these ends, does not this make mere expediency the ground upon which the State enacts and administers the law? In the same way it might be objected, that the Church, since it seeks man's eternal interests, acts upon a selfish principle. But we know that the highest end of the Church is God's honour and glory, yet we say nevertheless, that she seeks as her end, man's eternal interests, *i.e.*, it is her end in subordination to the still higher end. In the same way the State seeks man's temporal interests in accordance with the principles of natural justice. Or in other words, it puts the principles of natural justice above expediency, just as the Church puts the glory of God above the eternal interests of man.

2. *Church and State have different Constitutions.*

Both constitutions come from God, but they come in different ways. The one arises out of the natural wants of man, and he discovers it through these wants; the other is given by direct revelation to meet his spiritual wants. The Church has no visible head; the State must always have a visible head. The Lord Jesus, as we shall in due time prove from Scripture, is the only head of the Church; but He is not the only head of the State, for though He is King of kings, and over all, yet under Him, both Scripture and the constitutions of States recognize a visible head. The officers of the Church, as we have already seen, are of one order and of equal power, and do not exercise their power as individuals, but as members of assemblies or courts, the lower court being in subordination to the higher. In the State, officers are of different grades, and they do, on many occasions, exercise their power as individuals. The Scripture also points out the distinction between the grades of civil rulers and the equality of church officers. "Jesus called them unto him and said, Ye know that the princes of the Gentiles exercise dominion over them, and they that are great exercise authority upon them. But it shall not be so among you; but whosoever will be great among you, let him be your minister, and whosoever will be chief among you, let him be your servant." * The Church must neither add to, nor take from the laws which God has given her; † the State may make such laws as it thinks best to meet the wants of its subjects, provided always that it does not violate the laws of God. The Church binds its members to obey all the just laws of the State; the State does not bind its subjects to obey the Church.

The laws of the Church are not enforced in the same way as those of the State. In the case of the Church, the penalty of violating the law is invariably one of deprivation of privilege; it is not lawful for her to touch one of her members in either person or property; the State, on the other hand, enforces its laws by such penalties as deprivation of privilege, fine, imprisonment, and death. If you give to the Church such penalties as the latter, she at once goes beyond the power conferred on her, and introduces persecution, which is perfectly abhorrent to the entire spirit of Christianity. In fine, persuasion is a fundamental principle of the constitution of the latter, while force is a similar principle in the constitution of the former.

3. The officers of the Church require qualifications different from those required by the State's officers.

The officers of the Church require a thorough knowledge of Christianity, both theoretical and experimental, that they may be qualified to teach it, and to administer those laws which tend to its advancement. On the other hand, the officer of the State can perform his State duties without any experimental knowledge of Christianity: all he needs is natural religion and the knowledge of his particular department.

We have now seen that Church and State are distinct in everything which constitutes them societies or organi-

---

* Matt. xx, 25, 26, 27.   † See chap. IX.

zations of men: and so we conclude that they are entirely distinct and separate, and no officer of the one, as such, has any authority in the other.

We do not say that because one is a civil officer, that he is thereby disqualified from holding office in the Church. If he have time and qualifications, he may be appointed to perform duties as a church officer, but it is in virtue of his appointment as a church officer that he performs such duties, and not because of his power in civil matters. In the same way the church officer may be made a civil ruler. But two such offices should never be held by any, but those who have qualifications for both and time to perform the duties of both. This virtually shuts out the minister of the gospel from the civil office, for there is always more work for him in his own department than he can do, and therefore he should give himself wholly to it.

4. Those who amalgamate Church and State commit a great sin.

Not only does it appear that Church and State are distinct organizations, but it is a fact which cannot be denied, that just in proportion as they have been confounded, have mankind suffered. The Church of Rome has maintained that the State is only a phase of the Church, and the world has had from her many a sad lesson written in blood, by reason of the use she has made of the civil sword in propagating her damnable heresies. The Church of England gave herself up to the State, and the State has used her for its own purposes, at one time persecuting by her, at another, forcing her holiest and best officers and members to leave her, and all along protecting within her pale, all forms of heresy from out-and-out infidelity to Romanism. The Established Church of Scotland has been a more faithful witness for Christianity than either of the other two above-named, but still she has suffered much from her connection with the State, and even now she is trying to throw off her grievous burden.

The more progress liberty makes, and the more enlightened men become, the more clearly do they see the propriety and necessity of an entire separation of Church and State. As illustrating the above fact, we have the policy of Canada, Italy, and the United States; and last, but not the less significant, that of Britain in the case of the Irish Episcopal Church. The conduct of our own celebrated Prime Minister, the Right Hon. W. E. Gladstone, is a good illustration of what we have stated. When a young man, he wrote a work on Church and State, in which he set forth Erastianism in its most undisguised form; but in after life, when his mind became more enlightened and expanded, he carried through Parliament, the bill which made void the unholy alliance between Church and State in Ireland.

Of the four propositions which we enunciated at page 140, we have proved the last, and the other three of necessity fall to the ground. This should end the discussion of the subject, but there are some, who, while they maintain that the Church and State are separate institutions, hold, what seems to us, a doctrine contrary to this, namely, that the State is bound, at least in a measure, to support the Church. We shall now consider this doctrine.

State support and Voluntaryism.

If the view we have taken of the Church and State is the correct one, then it is a misappropriation of the funds of the State to give them to the Church. The State collects money avowedly for State purposes, and appropriates at least, a part of it, to Church purposes. But it may be said, the State collects some of its revenue with the declared intention of giving it to the Church. Then we say, the State must either look upon the Church as a part of its machinery, or give its money away for no end of its own. The former we have already shown to be wrong, and the latter, all must admit, is wrong. But still it is asked, is it not the duty of the State to teach morality, and is it not also a fact that the Church teaches morality; may not the Church then take payment from the State, when she does the work of the State? We reply, is it not the duty of the Church to teach morality, and does not the State also teach it; may the State then not demand payment from the Church for doing the work of the Church? The answer of common sense to both of these questions is, since both have to teach morality, let both teach it, and each support its own teachers. But again, says the objector, the Church can teach morality better than the State, and therefore the State wisely hands the work over to her. We answer, in as far as the State has to teach morality, it can do it much better than the Church, and therefore the State is unwise indeed in handing it over to the Church, while the latter goes out of her province altogether when she undertakes to teach morality for the State. That we may show the foundation upon which this last statement rests, let us here stop and inquire into the nature of Christianity, and its place, in as far as the good of our race is concerned.

On this subject, we fear there yet remains, among the great mass of the people, much confusion of thought, if we should not say plainly, ignorance. Many imagine that the recognition of the facts, that there is a God, that He has given us moral law, and that we are bound to obey that law, is part and parcel of Christianity; hence we often hear such arguments as these for the support of the Church, the teacher of *Christianity*, by the State, the teacher of *morality* in as far as its own ends are concerned. The civil ruler is bound to acknowledge God, and obey Him, and is he not therefore bound to recognize Christianity by adopting it as the State religion? or this, is the civil ruler not bound to conform, in the performance of all his duties, to the revealed will of Christ, and if so, is he not bound to teach Christianity for State purposes, and if bound in any way to teach it, what better instrumentality can he employ than the Church?

Nothing short of the truth could be more plausible; but still it is short of the truth, and therefore fallacious. It takes for granted that because the civil ruler is the "minister of God," that he is therefore the minister of Christianity; that because the civil ruler must conform to that part of the revealed will of Christ which bears upon his peculiar duties, that he must conform also to the revealed will of Christ in the propagation of Christianity. But what are the facts of the case? Man *without* Christianity knew the true God, and without Christianity might have retained the knowledge of Him. And notwithstanding that greatest of all calamities—the fall, man can retain the knowledge of a system of morality; and perhaps even where such knowledge has been lost, from the light of nature again develop it. The knowledge of God and morality then belongs to man as man, and not necessarily to man as a sinful being under a dispensation of grace.

Here then is the place which Christianity takes. When man fell, while he did not lose the knowledge of morality; he lost the power to practise morality, except as an outward form; but Christianity comes and gives men new spiritual life, so that they are able to begin the practice of morality, not as an outward form alone, but as an exercise of soul similar to that which Adam was capable of before he fell. Thus Christianity, not itself morality, incorporates morality, or in other words, it engrafts morality on to itself. But though the two thus become one, in the sense in which the tree and the branch grafted into it become one, they are nevertheless, two different things. Morality once grew in perfection without Christianity; and after man fell, the former could remain a perfect system for him to look at when he could no longer practise it aright, and it might also remain to produce in him such good works so called, as the unregenerate man can do: thus it is a manifestly different thing from Christianity.

To use another illustration, in which we shall make morality, not the twig, but the whole tree, and Christianity the quickening principle of the soil. Before man fell, the tree of morality grew in perfection in the soil of Adam's heart. The consequence of the fall was not the total destruction of that beautiful tree, but the injury of the soil, so that the tree in its perfection could not remain in it. The leaves, flowers, and fruit of holy practice were taken away, and nothing but the dead trunk of a system, with the naked limbs of works, which only have the form of what is good, not the spirit, remained. Christianity fertilizes the barren soil of the human heart, and that tree again springs into life and beauty, covered with the green leaves, flowers, and fruits of morality, carried out in the practice of souls in which the image of God has been restored. We see then, that the knowledge of morality, involving the knowledge of the one true God, and the practice of morality in as far as the State requires it, are things independent of Christianity; or in other words, natural religion and Christianity are different things, and the State requires nothing more for its purpose than natural religion.

We can now easily see the fallacy of such arguments as we alluded to a little while ago. The civil ruler is bound to acknowledge God and obey Him, and is he not therefore bound to recognize Christianity by adopting it as the State religion? which, stated in other words, amounts to this, is the civil ruler in his official capacity not bound, according to the principles of natural religion, to recognize God and obey Him, and therefore should such ruler not teach Christianity too? We see at once that the conclusion is a non-sequitur.

To take another objection: is the civil ruler not bound to conform, in the performance of all his duties, to the revealed will of Christ; and if so, is he not bound to teach Christianity for State purposes? In this argument two facts are concealed: 1st., that the revealed will of Christ includes both natural religion and

Christianity, and 2nd., that the civil ruler, in his official capacity, has only to do with the former.

The reader will here mark, that we do not teach that the State has nothing to do with the Bible; on the contrary, as it incorporates natural religion, it is the best book in which one can study the principles of that religion.

What we have brought forward in theory, the truth has, in spite of opposing theories, forced men to receive and act upon, as may be seen in the case of the Free Church of Scotland, and in that of the most enlightened civil governments of the age.

If again asked, why it should be so with Church and State in these matters, why the one goes no farther than the principles of natural religion in accomplishing its work, while the other must always teach Christianity to gain its end? We answer, it is necessary that man, in reference to certain temporal concerns, should be dealt with as man, *i.e.*, as a moral being under law and capable of breaking that law; and men, by the direction of God, have organized themselves into a State for this purpose; but for eternal interests (and in some measure for temporal interests), it is necessary that he be dealt with as a fallen being, under a dispensation of grace; and men, by the direction of God, have organized themselves into a Church for this purpose. Each society has a constitution which exactly fits it for its peculiar work, and the two societies together take up the whole field of the good of man, in as far as the good of individuals can be taken up by such societies.

Let us now return to that place where we left off to consider the nature of Christianity. We there made the statement, in answer to the assertion that the Church could teach morality better than the State, that in as far as the State had to teach morality, it could do it much better than the Church, while the latter went out of her place altogether, when she undertook to teach morality for the former.

We have already seen that the State teaches morality from the standpoint of natural religion. It holds up as a reward to the keepers of its laws, the enjoyment of natural rights; but how can the Church do such a thing, when she has no power to secure for men their natural rights? It inflicts upon the breakers of its laws, such punishment as is in accordance with the principles of natural justice, but how can the Church do this, when she has no power to inflict corporal punishment upon any one? This is the State's first great lesson in morality, and the Church cannot possibly teach it at all. In the second place, it is the duty of the State to afford its subjects such knowledge as shall enable them to live as becomes good citizens; but in no case does it require anything more than an outward conformity to its own laws, not even to all moral law, for we have already seen that it does not take notice of many outward violations of moral law. Part of the knowledge just mentioned, is afforded by the laws of the State; how then can the Church undertake to give such knowledge; can she take upon herself to say what the laws of the State are? But suppose the State to put into her hands, its laws and statutes, and out of these and such moral laws, as it is always well known that the former enforces, she were to construct a new bible, and go forth, would not hers then be a glorious mission! Does the Church then undertake to teach the first great lesson for the State, she becomes a persecutor; does she undertake to teach the second, she stoops from her high and peculiar position—she lets go of Christianity for civil law and natural religion? The State teaches simply a doctrine of good works in as far as the ends of the State are concerned; the Church teaches that there must be union with Christ and a change of heart, before any good works in the highest sense can be performed—that it is union with Christ and regeneration, which lay the foundation for all proper action on the part of man as a creature of God. In a word, she must always seek the cultivation of morality through this union with Christ, if she succeeds in persuading men to accept of Christ, then she may teach them moral law with some hope that they can obey it, at least in part. If then she stoops to teach morality for the State, she must either give up this lofty position, or teach in her own way, backed by State power and State weapons, which is contrary both to the teachings of Christ and the dictates of human reason: for we rebel at the thought of having even the religion of Christ forced upon us, as we may be forced to serve in war, or pay a tax. This kind of force has never yet accomplished anything for Christianity, and it is not the design of Christ that it should: it is true here, that "They that take the sword shall perish with the sword."* The Christian religion is one propagated by persuasion, not by force, and the only sword is the "sword of the Spirit which is the word of God."†

I may be told here, that I have mistaken altogether the position of those who maintain that the State should support the Church without controlling it: the advocates of this doctrine never thought of the Church's leaving her own peculiar position. But we repeat, she must, if she accept State support, either leave her own position, or propagate religion by the power of the civil sword. If this has not been made plain enough already, we shall yet do so. But let us hear in full the apology for State support. The Church, while teaching in her own peculiar way, improves the morals of the community,— makes crime less, and consequently helps the State, and therefore, the latter should pay her. In doing all this, I ask, has she done anything more than her duty, anything more than Christ requires of her? Certainly not. Does she then demand pay for doing what it is her duty to do without such pay? An argument just as sound and as forcible can be made in behalf of Church support for the State. The State while teaching morality in its own way, establishes order in the community, protects the rights of

---

* Math. xxvi, 52   † Eph. vi, 17.

citizens, and allows them to meet as members of the Church, none daring to make them afraid, and in short helps the Church greatly: for this help the State should be paid by the Church. This argument is every whit as sound and as plausible as the one preceding it. The fact is, each should do its duty, and support itself; and for either to demand payment of the other for performing its own peculiar duty, is preposterous. We have already shown that they should not, and cannot undertake each other's duties, as each is fitted only for the performance of its own.

From another and independent point of view, it appears that the Church should not accept of State support. It must appear plain to all, that God has not committed the preaching of the Gospel to man, because He could not find other agents to do the work. He who had no need of Peter's sword, had as little need of Peter's voice. But for man's own benefit the Lord gave him such service to perform. All who assist in any way in publishing the gospel, are therefore benefited as well as those to whom it is published. It follows then, that there should be, first, a willingness on our part to do the work of the the Church ourselves rather than to shift it upon any one else, and secondly, that we, in getting the help of others in this great work, should get it in such a way as to benefit, in the first place, our helpers, *i.e.*, in a word, to make Christians of them. If we had charge of the physical education of a child, it would be necessary for us, not only to give it the proper kinds of food, but also to provide exercise for it; and that exercise should not be that to which we must drive it with the lash, but such as it would itself delight to engage in. The Church has charge of the spiritual education of man, and must not only supply the proper spiritual food, but also provide spiritual exercise for him. He must not be forced to engage in this exercise, otherwise it would do him no good but harm. The child might be forced to take physical exercise, and still that exercise would do him some good; but the child has only one body to cultivate, while man has two dispositions, and a service which, if engaged in willingly, would cultivate the good disposition, if forced upon the same individual, will cultivate the evil one. The service which one performs in contributing of his substance for the support of the gospel, is no exception to the above. Every one who gives from right motives, freely and of his own accord, is blessed in the giving,—his soul is enlarged; while every one who is forced to give, feels that he has been oppressed, and his soul is stirred with indignation against the oppressor. Hence we have such passages in the Bible as these, " Every man according as he purposeth in his heart, so let him give; not grudgingly nor of necessity: for God loveth a cheerful giver."* "It is more blessed to give than to receive."†

The Church must then see to it, that all funds for her support are raised so as to benefit, in the first place, those who contribute to them. But when she accepts support from the State, she does something far different from this: she says in effect, I cannot get enough money for my support in the way in which my Lord indicates that I should get it, viz., from the free-will offerings of men; but you, the State, can always have as much as you need, for you have power to force men to pay, will you not then give a portion of your revenue to me? Does the Church not in this matter ask the aid of the civil sword? Most undoubtedly she does. She knows full well that there is not an established church in Christendom which does not every year receive money that has been paid through force, if for no other reason than this, that it was going to her. And there is not a member of an established church in existence, who can say from his heart, I would willingly and cheerfully pay the tax if my church were disestablished, and that of my dissenting neighbour put in its place. But even though all the

---

* II Cor. ix, 7.   † Acts xx, 35.

members of the Church in the land, were of one denomination, and there was not a single dissenter, it would be wrong to call for their services in any way except in that which would cultivate their spiritual natures. In a word, it would be wrong to force any to give, when Christ desires nothing but voluntary offerings.

We have now fulfilled the promise which we made a few pages back, by showing that the highest ground which can possibly be taken in favour of State support, involves the use of State weapons on behalf of the Church.

CHRIST IS IN EVERY SENSE THE HEAD OF THE CHURCH.

That the Lord Jesus is the head of the Church, and the head too in every sense, is clearly taught in the Scriptures. "*He is the head of the body, the church;* who is the beginning, the firstborn from the dead; that *in all things* he might have the preëminence."* Again we are informed, that God "hath put all things under his feet and gave him to be the head over all things to the church, which is his body, the fulness of him that filleth all in all."† In the same epistle from which the above is quoted, Paul tells us that a ministry has been given to the Church, not that all its members may be brought under the sway of an earthly ruler, but "For the perfecting of the saints, for the work of the ministry, for the edifying of the body of Christ: Till we all come in the unity of the faith, and of the knowledge of the Son of God, unto a perfect man, unto the measure of the stature of the fulness of Christ: That we henceforth be no more children, tossed to and fro, and carried about with every wind of doctrine, by the sleight of men, and cunning craftiness, whereby they lie in wait to deceive; But speaking the truth in love, may grow up into him in all things, which is the head, even Christ: From whom

---

* Col. i, 18.   † Eph. i, 22, 23.

the whole body fitly joined together and compacted by that which every joint supplieth, according to the effectual working in the measure of every part, maketh increase of the body unto the edifying of itself in love."* Christ Himself, when speaking of the weakness of the Scribes and Pharisees in wishing to be called *Rabbi, Rabbi*, says to His disciples, "But be not ye called Rabbi, for one is your Master even Christ; and all ye are brethren. And call no man your father upon the earth, for one is your Father which is in heaven. Neither be ye called masters for one is your Master even Christ."† When He commissioned His disciples saying, "Go ye therefore and teach all nations," &c., He did not say, I have appointed one to oversee you, and direct you; but He said, "Lo I am with you alway even unto the end of the world. Amen."‡ When He apppeared unto John in Patmos, He did not say, My vicar has charge of you, but He said, "These things saith he that holdeth the seven stars" (the ministers) "in his right hand, who walketh in the midst of the seven golden candlesticks"§ (the churches).

We have now found that the pope is not the head of the Church, that the civil magistrate is not the head of it, and that Christ is the head of it. And why should any one doubt or hesitate for a moment in recognizing Him as her head in every sense, for there is no objection which can be brought forward which our doctrine of the Headship of Christ does not fully and effectually meet. We may be told of our want of unity, of authority, and all that, but with Christ for our head, we have all the unity and authority which the Church can desire. Some may give us what they think are grand notions of the Church —notions which remind us of nothing so much as of the vessel which Peter saw in a vision let down from heaven to earth, "wherein were all manner of four-footed beasts

---

* Eph. iv, 12–16.   † Matth. xxiii, 8–10.
‡ Math. xxviii, 19, 20.   § Rev. ii, 1.

of the earth, and wild beasts, and creeping things, and fowls of the air,"* but with these essential differences: Peter's vessel was let down from heaven; the so-called church is an ark manufactured on earth; all that was in Peter's vessel was put there and cleansed by God; all that is found in this ark has been put there by man, and a great part of it has never been cleansed by any but man. "Behold our great ark," say they, "and behold upon *our* shoulders the keys by which it is opened and shut. It shall one day be taken up to heaven and all within it, and none but those within it shall go. Make haste to us, that we may open its doors for you, and then, and not till then, are you safe." From these blasphemers we turn away to One who calls from heaven, from the seat of highest authority, "The government is upon my shoulder,"† and " I open and none shall shut; and shut, and none shall open."‡ " Behold I have set before thee an open door, and no man can shut it."§ "I am the door‖ to My Church, which is not a great ark united to me by a single strand, but is a great company of saved ones, united to Me because each individual in it is united to Me by a vital union such as exists between the head¶ and members of the natural body; or such as subsists between the vine and its branches.** I have a work for this great company to do, and therefore I have organized it; but that work is not to attempt to wash away sins, but to publish the truth to a world lying in wickedness and sin, so that all who choose may find Me who alone can cleanse from sin; not to attempt the opening and shutting of heaven, but to teach and to warn by the Word and discipline, so that all who profess to know My name, may be aware of that for which *I* open and shut heaven."

We may be taunted too with our want of unity by those who are ever forward to point us to their own supposed

---

*Acts x, 12.   † Is. ix, 6.   ‡ Ibid xxii, 22.   § Rev. iii, 8.
‖ John x, 7–9.   ¶ I Cor, xii, 12, 27.   ** John xv, 1–6.

perfections in this respect. We, and we alone, have unity, they exclaim; everywhere we acknowledge the same visible head, everywhere we celebrate the same sacraments, everywhere the same prayers are offered, &c., &c.; while you are divided into ten thousand different sects, and cannot agree among yourselves as to anything.

We acknowledge at once that these parties have a unity not possessed by us. There was unity in the fact that all the different creatures which Peter saw were in one vessel, and a similar unity have they. But there was a unity in the things that Peter saw which they do not possess—those things were all cleansed of God. In this then their boasted unity consists,—a visible church in which are all manner of disciples, and in which all manner of doctrines are taught; in one visible church made up of Jesuits, Jansenists, believers in the infallibility of the pope, unbelievers in it, those who can believe everything and know nothing, and those who do not believe anything except that all religion is humbug. They have indeed all manner of doctrines except the truth. Where, we ask those of the Church of England who are so fond of copying Rome, and of putting their trust in the same vanities, is your boasted unity? You have your Calvinists, your Arminians, your Socinians, your Broad-church, High-church and Low-church, your Pantheists and infidels, and you are never tired of speaking of the comprehensiveness of your vessel to contain all manner of teachers and disciples. Is the unity not in the vessel alone? It is surely in the vessel, not in the contents. You have such a unity, and we have it not; but we have a unity, and we shall now tell you wherein it consists.

Our company is made up of all who are united to Christ, no matter in what denomination they are found; we claim the members of *the* Church from Independents, Baptists, Methodists, and many others, from Presbyterians, Episcopalians, and even from the Church of Rome. Much as you may dislike to have any of your people associated with us, still we shall not give up our claim. Here then is our unity; we have one Lord or Head, Jesus Christ; one faith, faith in Him; one baptism, baptism by His Holy Spirit; one God and Father of all.* We are fellow-soldiers in the same great army, have the same battles to fight, are led by the same Commander, look to the same common home, and expect to receive our laurels from the same kingly hand. Does not all this constitute unity in spite of denominational differences?

Permit us to employ an illustration. On the 25th of October, 1854, in the far distant Crimea, a great number of spectators, among whom was the Commander-in-chief of the British army, looked down from an eminence on squadrons marshalling below. A great mass of Muscovite cavalry approaching attracts every eye. There is in their way a long thin line of footmen whose peculiar dress tells of dear old Scotland's rugged mountains. The Muscovite is even now bearing down upon them. Why stand they thus so motionless? are they not going to form square for the terrible charge? Not they. In a moment the rattle of the rifle tells of their determination. On come the Russian horsemen, and another volley has decided the contest, for they turn and fly; and now the spectators send forth their rapturous shouts, "Bravo Highlanders! well done!" But in another moment the British cavalry must meet that approaching tide of horsemen. Right on and at them, sword in hand, go Enniskillen and Scots Greys to cut their desperate way through squadrons tenfold greater than their own. They succeed amid ringing cheers, and after them follow hard the 4th Royal Irish, the 6th Dragoon Guards, and the 1st Royal Dragoons, and finish the work of slaughter and victory.

Now who will say that because there were regimental differences here, there was no unity? Not

---

* Ep. iv, 4—6.

one of all these regiments, nor of all the others which
took part on that day, made a single happy thrust, but
that the same hearts rejoiced, and the same voices cheer-
ed. And why all this? Was it not because they had one
great and common work to do? Was it not because they
all obeyed one commander-in-chief, and all hoped some day
to return to the same shores, to meet the same glad wel-
come, to hear the same triumphant pœans, and to receive
their laurels from the same sovereign's hand? Were they
not then a united host?

We have only to change the scene to another battle-
field. There are mustered on it, various regiments, some
old and others recently formed. Their uniforms are different, their banners are different, and though on all the
banners there are the names of some fields of fame, there
are also on each, fields, in the glories of which, but a few
shared. There is the Methodist regiment. Its banner
bears the name of fields not usually found in records of
war, but I shall give some of them a place here: Canadian Backwoods, American Prairies, Islands of the Pacific,
and in civil strife renowned, it has gained victories in
England itself. There too is the Baptist regiment
with a long and proud roll; and not less renowned
is its companion in arms, the Independent. There
too is the Church of England regiment, and well may
it be proud of its record, for it has shared in many a
glorious victory; and among other things, has had the
greatest share in liberating England from the fellest tyrant
that has ever bound a fetter upon man. And shall
we fail to speak of our own, with its blue banner which
it has so often held aloft in spite of kings; under which it
has vowed to struggle to the death for that liberty wherewith Christ makes His people free, and in token of its stern
determination, has recorded its vows in blood; under
which it has driven back the mitred emissaries of a persecuting and bloody church, and rescued Scotland from
him in whose skirts shall be "found the blood of prophets

and of saints, and of all that were slain upon the earth."*
And there are others in this army that are of less note, but time fails us to speak of them.

Now all these fight one great battle, and the spectators which rejoice in the triumphs of one, also rejoice in the triumphs of all the others, for all the triumphs go to make the one great victory at which both heaven and earth rejoice. All obey the same Commander-in-chief, all look to the same final resting-place, all wait for the same triumphant song, all look for a "well done" from the same heavenly King, and expect to receive their laurels from His hand. And with their armour off and their decorations on, all shall at last join in the same hymns of praise to the great Leader who has brought them safely through.

It is true, that occasionally in times when there is a moment's leisure, some one of one regiment may criticise the organization of another regiment, or point out advantages which the army might gain by a different course on the part of some regiments, even as we do in this little book; but because we do so, it is no more to be supposed that we undervalue the services of other regiments, and think our own to be all in all, than it is to be supposed, that an officer who writes a book for the purpose of improving the organization of the army to which he belongs, imagines that his favourite regiment is the only part of it which can be depended on.

Now we ask, which unity is the best,—that which consists in putting the same uniforms on factious and quarrelsome companies, whose swords are ever being turned against each other, and in having them, as if to increase the quarrelling, all huddled into one mass; or that which consists in having regiments, with all their regimental peculiarities, united under one great Commander, whom they willingly follow, and for whom they are all willing to lay down their lives? The former is the unity of Rome, and

---

* Rev. viii, 24.

of those who copy her; the latter is the unity of Evangelical Protestantism. Oh, says the Papist, our bond of unity is visible to the world, and yours is not visible to any. We answer, for it holds true here, "The things which are seen are temporal, and the things which are not seen are eternal."

We may be told that we have no authority to say what the truth is. We reply, we have the best authority, Christ Himself, our head. If answered, that it is idle to say that Christ is our authority, as all acknowledge that He is, but what is wanted is some one to make us understand what Christ has taught; then we say, this is a work beyond the power of mortals. The pope may claim to infallibly interpret the truth; but his interpretations, his friends being judges, cannot be more infallible than the writings of Paul, Peter, or any other inspired man; and as men have differed as to what these have taught, are they not just as likely to differ about the pope's interpretations? Such interpretations are clearly not the remedy for man's want of understanding in the Scriptures, for this want of understanding arises, not from the fact that the Bible is, intellectually viewed, an obscure book, for in this sense it is the plainest of all books. The same doctrine is sometimes set forth in it in fifty different ways, and in the best ways, too, in order to reach the human understanding. The vision has indeed been made plain upon tables, that he may run that readeth it.* It is true, that of some passages in some parts of it, it has been said by an inspired writer, they are "things hard to be understood, which they that are unlearned and unstable, wrest as they do also the other scriptures unto their own destruction."† But who are the unlearned? Certainly not those who have little intellectual learning, for that would make such learning the touch-stone by which the truths of Scripture can be known. Yet we know it to be a fact, that many of the most learned men have misun-

---

* Hab. ii, 2.   † II Peter iii, 16.

derstood the Bible, and wrested it to their own destruction; while many of those who have had but little intellectual cultivation, have become wise unto salvation. This fact cannot be disputed by any, as we have divine authority for it: Jesus says, " I thank thee, O Father, Lord of heaven and earth, because thou hast hid these things from the wise and prudent, and hast revealed them unto babes."* Nor can the pope say that he is better able, because of his intellectual learning, to interpret the Scriptures, than many of those whom he has excommunicated. What then is the learning referred to by Peter? It is that which is gained through the teaching of the Spirit. We conclude then that the Bible is misunderstood, not from its being an obscure book, but from the fact that it requires the teaching of the Spirit to guarantee the reception of its truths. Even so it says itself, " The natural man receiveth not the things of the Spirit of God: for they are foolishness unto him: neither can he know them because they are spiritually discerned."† Now the remedy for this state of things is not to be found in even a divinely inspired pope, for what could he give us better than the inspired writings which we have, and the natural man understands them not? Nor is it to be found in a pope taught by the Spirit in any way, for if raised from spiritual death by that Spirit's quickening influence, it no more gives the pope power to impart the same life to another, than the fact that Christ raised up Lazarus, gave the latter power to raise others from the dead.

Here is the remedy. " It is written in the prophets: and they shall be all taught of God," (i. e. all the members of the Christian Church as may be seen by comparing Is. liv., with Gal. iv., 21, 31)—" Every man therefore that hath heard and hath learned of the Father, cometh unto me."‡ Again, " If any man will do his will he shall know of the doctrine, whether it be of God or

---

* Math. xi, 25.   † I Cor. ii, 14.   ‡ John vi, 45.

whether I speak of myself."* Now it is through Christ that we know the Father, and the Father's will; and it is through Christ that we get the Spirit by whom we are taught of God; hence for the right understanding of Scripture, all are referred directly to Christ the head of the Church, and not to the pope, or to any human authority.

It may be objected that we have our Confession of Faith as an authority; but the Confession of Faith is not an authoritative document intended to bind the conscience of any man, it is a basis of agreement upon which a number of God's people unite as a denomination (as explained at page 15), for the better accomplishment of the Lord's work. We do not say of him who refuses to receive each and every statement which it contains, "Let him be anathema," but of those who refuse to receive some of its statements, we simply say, they are not Presbyterians, and of others who reject them all, that they are heathens or infidels.

It may also be objected, that we have a ministry which exercises authority in the Church; true, but we claim that over that ministry, there is no head but Christ, and that in the exercise of authority, its members can go no farther than His revealed will, as we shall endeavour to show in the following chapter, hence all the private members of the Church can demand of them a warrant from Christ for any act of power on their part, and they, in turn, while binding and loosing in the name of Christ and by His authority will have their acts ratified in heaven; and so of the ministry, it holds true, and not of the pope, that whatsoever it shall bind on earth, shall be bound in heaven, and whatsoever it shall loose on earth shall be loosed in heaven.

The ministers do not claim that their teaching is infallible. They allow all who hear them to test what they say by the Word of God, and like Paul, they call those

---

* John vii, 17.

noble who do so. They declare plainly that he who would fully understand whether their preaching is true or not must be taught of God, so as to realize the fulfilment of the promise of Christ, "If any man will do His will he shall know of the doctrine, whether it be of God or whether I speak of myself." They know that they are liable to make mistakes, but as it has "pleased God by the foolishness of preaching to save them that believe,"* they preach what they think is the truth, after they have taken the same course to discover it which they recommend to others, and leave the results with Him. Thus notwithstanding the fact that we have a Confession of Faith and a ministry, the members of the Church, for the reception of the truth, are left with the head of the Church.

So Christ, we see, is head of the Church in every sense. And why should He not be? Why should pope or civil ruler dare to come between the soul and its God. To Christ alone in matters of conscience we must give account, and in such matters He alone must be our master. The civil ruler may think that as he should control all things for the good of the people under him, that he should also have control of so great an instrumentality for good as the Church most certainly is. But this will always be found true, that the ruler who takes to himself power to which he has no right (and we have shown that the civil ruler has no authority in the Church), even for the purpose of doing good, will entirely fail. While at the same time, he who keeps his place and leaves the headship of the Church to Him to whom it belongs, will find that he is more benefited by it when thus free, than he could possibly be, by dragging it captive at the chariot wheels of the State.

---

* I Cor. i, 21.

CHAPTER IX.

THE DIVINE RIGHT OF THE SCRIPTURAL FORM OF CHURCH GOVERNMENT.

THOUGH one might admit, that we have been perfectly successful in developing from the Scriptures a complete form of Church Government, he might still ask us to show him that it is the form which all are bound to adopt. This we now undertake to do.

The Romanist, Episcopalian, and some others, try with all their strength to prove that their several forms are scriptural. And it is only when they fail in their vain attempts, that they declare in disgust, either that the Scriptures do not teach any form at all, or else, if they do, that it is not binding upon all. But we cannot help thinking, that the very fact that they try so hard to prove their systems scriptural, is a tacit admission that the scriptural system is binding.

Of all who have tried it, we think that Hooker has made the ablest defence of the Episcopal system of Church Government, and here follows a summing up of his views:—" What the Church of God standeth bound to know or do, the same in part nature teacheth. And because nature can teach them but only in part, neither so fully as is requisite for man's salvation, nor so easily as to make the way plain and expedite enough that many may come to the knowledge of it, and so be saved; therefore in Scripture hath God both collected the most necessary things that the school of nature teacheth unto that end, and revealed also whatsoever we neither could with safety be ignorant of, nor at all be instructed in but by supernatural revelation from him. So that Scripture containing all things that are in this kind any way needful for the Church, and the principal of the other sort, this is the next thing wherewith we are charged as with an error: we teach that whatsoever is unto salvation termed *necessary* by way of excellency, whatsoever it standeth all men upon to know or do that they may be saved, whatsoever there is whereof it may truly be said, 'this not to believe is eternal death and damnation,' or, 'this every soul that will live must duly observe,' of which sort the articles of Christian faith and the sacraments of the Church of Christ are. All such things, if Scripture did not comprehend, the Church of God should not be able to measure out the length and breadth of that way wherein forever she is to walk, heretics and schismatics never ceasing, some to abridge, some to enlarge, all to pervert and obscure the same. But as for those things that are accessory hereunto, those things that so belong to the way of salvation as to alter them is no otherwise to change that way, than a path is changed by altering only the uppermost face thereof; which, be it laid with gravel or set with grass, or paved with stone, remaineth still the same path. In such things, because discretion may teach the Church what is convenient, we hold not the Church further tied herein unto Scripture, than that against Scripture nothing be admitted in the Church, lest that path which ought always to be kept even, do thereby come to be overgrown with brambles and thorns."* How many, who at the outset had scruples not a few respecting the polity of the Episcopal Church, and who having wearily plodded through Hooker's work, at last, with

---

* Ecc. Pol., p. 291, B. 3, Ch. 3, Sec. 3.

great satisfaction, rested on this oasis. Even Hooker himself seems to draw breath here and exclaims in triumph, "If this be unsound, wherein doth the point of unsoundness lie?"* Where doth the point of unsoundness lie? Who is able to discover such a point, after all that learned discussion upon laws, which so clearly shows us what we never doubted, that, as the law of nature is in some things a sufficient guide for us, God has not in these things given us any other guide, and hence we need not expect to find a direct warrant in the Bible for everything. So we think after all that Hooker has laboured in vain, teaching us what we already knew perfectly well, and leaving all our difficulties, with respect to the polity of his church, untouched. Where is the point of unsoundness? "*We hold not the Church further tied herein unto Scripture, than that against Scripture nothing be admitted in the Church,*" lest the way of salvation be too much altered, nay even to the planting of thorns and brambles in it. But might it not have occurred to Hooker, that what would be to his tough feet, grass, might to another, prove thorns and brambles; that what might be to him but a paved walk or a paved way, might be a way full of stumbling blocks and rocks of offence to others. 'Nevertheless,' says Hooker, 'the Church is not to be held further tied herein unto Scripture, than that against Scripture nothing be admitted in the Church,' *i.e.* whatever is not forbidden by the Scripture is permitted.

That this principle does not admit of universal application, we are convinced as soon as we hear it stated; that it does admit of a restricted application, we are also sure, whenever we get the particular example which illustrates it. Grant it in its widest sense, and at once the way is open for the inventions of men in the worship of God, *i.e.* for will-worship; deny it in every particular, and at once we must find a warrant in the Scriptures, either

---

* Ecc. Pol., B. 3, Ch. 3. Sec. 4.

direct or implied, for everything that we would do. We must then discover in what it applies, and in what it does not.

THE PRINCIPLE "WHATEVER IS NOT FORBIDDEN IS PERMITTED" TESTED.

1. In reference to individuals regulating their own conduct.

All laws are given to us either as general rules or exceptions : *e.g.*, God said to Noah, and through him to all his descendants, " Every moving thing that liveth shall be meat for you."* This is a law for us at the present day, a general rule let us call it. But we have laws which are exceptions to it, the game laws for instance ; at such and such times, say they, you must not kill deer, take particular kinds of fish, and so on. It will be found that all our laws are in this way either general rules or exceptions : and exceptions themselves may be viewed as general rules to other exceptions under them. Now it will appear clear, that the principle "Whatever is not forbidden is permitted or sanctioned" is true or false according to the nature of the law to which it is applied. If the general rule be one of permission or sanction, and the exception one of prohibition, then it is true in reference to the exception, that " *Whatever is not forbidden is permitted or sanctioned.* If the general rule is *to take everything that moveth*, and the exception, *you must not take deer*, then in virtue of the general rule, whatever is not prohibited by the exception is permitted. But on the other hand if the general rule be one of prohibition, and the exception one of permission, it will follow that whatever is not permitted by the exception, is prohibited by the general rule, and hence we have a canon just the opposite of the one already stated, viz., *Whatever is not sanctioned is prohibited.* E.G., as a general rule

---
* Gen. ix, 3.

God prohibited the marriage of a woman with her deceased husband's brother, but as an exception to this, when the husband had died without children, he made it the duty of the deceased husband's brother to marry his sister-in-law, in order to raise up his brother's name. Thus far the exception went; but beyond the exception the brother must not go; if the deceased husband had left children, the marriage could not take place. Or to take another example: the general rule is, "Thou shall not kill," and let us for brevity's sake, say the exception is, you may kill to defend your own life. Is it not clear that whatever is not sanctioned here by the exception is prohibited by the general rule? We have now found that there are two canons instead of one to be applied in this way to laws, and which one we ought to apply, must be determined by the nature of the laws to which we would apply them.

The law in dispute is that which relates to the worship and service of God. To this law does the former or latter canon apply? We can get at the truth here by inquiring how the law regulating the worship and service of God as revealed in the Bible stands in relation to the more general law. But what is the more general law? Hooker would say the law of nature. Now the law of nature teaches us that we are under the strongest obligations to worship God; but the law of Christian worship, though it contains many obligations, none will deny, is, in general, one of permission. But why permit that by a specially revealed law, which is already enforced by the more general law? It is here that Hooker has missed that law which he would have done well to consider, and which would have enabled him to understand his opponents, a thing which he never appeared to do. Had man never fallen, the law of nature, for aught we know, would have been all the law which we ever should have needed, but as soon as man fell by reason of sin, a law at once went forth prohibiting him any approach to his Maker. (We may call it, *the law of spiritual death.*) Nor do we find that he attempted it, until he again got liberty; on the contrary, he fled from his Maker, and hid himself. Though the law of nature still taught him his obligations to worship God, yet he, being under condemnation, was as effectually shut out from access to God as the devils now are.

It may, by the unthinking, be said, how absurd to speak of the law of nature as imposing a universal obligation, and at the same time of another law which bars the way to the performance of that obligation. But do we not find analogous things in the Scriptures themselves? Is it not laid down there as man's duty, to turn from his sins and live, while we are told that he is dead in sin; now this operation of the law of spiritual death prevents his leaving his sins; nevertheless the obligation is the same. He is called upon to awake from his sleep and arise from the dead, but how can he raise himself from the dead? Do not the devils also know that they are under obligation to serve God, and yet on account of their sin they neither can, nor must they presume to seek God's face. Then we say, notwithstanding the obligations of the law of nature, that the fall of man effectually bars the way of access to God, by reason of that law which must ever so separate the condemned sinner from his Creator. But it may be objected, while it is man's duty to arise from the death of sin, he being unable to do so, God puts forth power to enable him to rise. Yes, but it is equally the duty of those for whom God does not put forth his power; and after all, God in putting forth His power, just does an exceptional thing which removes the barrier, and so here, God, by revealing to us a way of salvation, does an exceptional thing which removes the barrier in the way of access to Him. We need not say, in this connection, anything more of the obligation of the law of nature, but confine our attention to the other two, viz., *that which bars the way of access* to God, and that which is an exception to it. *the law for the worship and service of God under*

Christianity.* Now the general rule here is one of prohibition, and the particular, one of permission, hence it follows, that whatever is not permitted by the law regulating the worship and service of God under Christianity, is prohibited by the more general law; and a canon exactly the opposite of the Episcopalian's applies, viz., *Whatever is not sanctioned is prohibited.*

It may however still be asked, if such is the case, must you not find sanction in the Bible for everything which you do? Yes, in one sense we must, and in another we need not: we must find sanction for every act of worship, formal or otherwise, but not for everything which we do. This arises from the fact, that Christianity is the basis or footing upon which we enjoy natural privileges in religion. As soon as Adam fell, he forfeited every privilege which the law of nature gave him, though he did not escape from its obligations. What natural privilege could he have enjoyed after he had fallen, without Christianity? What natural privilege could he have enjoyed, unless "the Lamb slain from the foundation of the world,"† had delivered him from going down to the pit? But as soon as the Redeemer had said, "Lo, I come; in the volume of the book it is written of me, I delight to do thy will, O my God,"‡ the law of Christianity prevailed: and upon this law, and upon this law alone as a foundation, the privileges allowed by natural law were enjoyed. Thus Christianity came, having, as it were, the blessings given by natural law embodied in it. Now since Christianity thus incorporates our natural rights, there are certain things permitted to us in virtue of the law of nature based on Christianity, for which we are not required to find a warrant in the Bible.

---

* The reader must not suppose that Christianity was not introduced until Christ came in the flesh. It was introduced when the Lord God made known that the seed of the woman should bruise the head of the serpent, for in this bruising of the serpent's head He pointed out a way of deliverance to man.

† Rev. xiii, 8. ‡ Ps. xl, 7, 8.

Wherein does this differ from Hooker, it may be asked? In this: we do not make the law of nature in religion wider than the basis upon which we are permitted to enjoy its privileges; while Hooker and his followers do so. They contend, *e.g.*, that we may use any forms in religious service not forbidden by the Bible; we maintain, that we are allowed only to use such as are, from the nature of things, or in other words, according to the law of nature, necessary attendants upon the act of worship sanctioned or required by the law of Christianity: and this too for the reason given, that we must not make the superstructure, natural rights, wider than the basis, the law of Christianity. Hooker and his followers would say, *e.g.*, since the Bible does not forbid such things as, the sign of the cross in baptism, the turning of the face to the altar, at a particular stage of the service, or the bowing of the head at another, that we may employ them in accordance with the light of nature; we say, since no act of Christian worship necessarily requires these or any other similar forms that we must not use them.

But in order to show more clearly how far we think the law of nature may be allowed to direct us, let us take an illustration: man, as a condemned sinner without hope, must not venture to approach God in prayer, but as soon as salvation is made known, prayer is permitted. How then is it in reference to standing, kneeling, sitting, lying, or walking, while praying? We say, since God has permitted prayer, and has not given us any direction as to the particular position which we shall take when we pray, or as to the exact words or forms of expression which we shall use; then the position and forms of expression are not significant of anything in worship, and may be such as the law of nature teaches as becoming; but if, in connection with prayer, He instructs Cain and Abel to sacrifice a lamb, the firstling of the flock, without blemish; then the offering of that sacrifice is a significant form of worship, and nothing but a lamb, the firstling of the flock and without blemish, will do : here then the canon, which we have found applies to such things, has full force, viz., whatever is not sanctioned is prohibited.

Those who are bent on finding objections rather than truth, may here ask, what do you mean by not making the law of nature in religion wider than the basis upon which the enjoyment of its privileges rests? You tell us that it is through Christianity that we enjoy natural rights. Do you mean to say that unless we get a warrant in the Scriptures as a foundation for it, we are not to breathe the air, partake of food, wear clothing, cultivate the land, or do any such thing? Such a question is really no objection at all, for it implies a complete want of understanding in the subject under consideration. We say that Christianity is a religion suited to men who have forfeited every right, both religious and natural; without it, they must have been swept down to the pit. But as soon as a scheme of salvation was made known, it brought along with it, of necessity, natural blessings, such as life, the liberty to use the means of sustaining life, to wit, air, water, food, clothing, sleep, and exercise—in fine, the privilege of doing anything and everything which tend to give this life the best possible development, while it taught the avoiding of everything which tends to hinder such development. For what use would it be to a rebel under sentence of death to receive a pardon on certain conditions, if he be not allowed to live long enough to ascertain what they are, in order to accept them and save his life? Even so Christianity would be of no use, unless life be granted to men to make themselves acquainted with its nature, that they may see whether they will accept it or not.

Now for what object should life thus preserved be sustained and developed—to build some great temple for the reception of images of what man might conceive to be the great Creator and Redeemer, and to bow down and worship these images, or to practise the rites of any other religion which man might invent? No! but for this and this alone, the reception and practice of Christianity, since it was for the reception and practice of Christianity that physical life and its blessings were given. From what has just been said, it follows, that we make natural privileges no wider than the basis upon which they rest, when we make use of life and all its blessings for the cultivation of Christianity; and we do make them wider, when we use them in the practice of any religion except the Christian.

Since then it is evident that our life has been given us for the reception and practice of Christianity, it behooves us to know what it is, and accordingly we turn to the Revelation where it is found. And in it, let us say that we find the privilege of prayer granted, and no particular position which we are to take when praying specified. Then the very fact that our natural life has been given us for the practice of Christianity, just opens the way for such natural acts as are necessary for the performance of the duty* and the enjoyment of the privilege. Now we make the law of nature in religion no wider than the basis upon which it rests, when in worship, we go no farther on its authority than to perform those things which are necessary attendants upon a specified act of Christian worship. But when we use, *e.g.*, the sign of the cross in baptism, we have a form not specified in the Christian system; and besides, one which is not a necessary attendant upon any act of Christian worship, for it would be absurd to say, "baptism cannot be performed without some such sign." And hence, if we claim that the light of nature teaches us to use this sign, we make use of our natural privileges to practice something which is not in Christianity, and so make the privileges of the

---

* The reader will bear in mind that while we have been regarding Christianity as a religion of privilege or permission, because our argument only requires this view, we are not overlooking the fact that it is also a religion of duty. The very fact that it is a religion of privilege, makes it from the nature of things, a religion of duty.

law of nature in religion wider than the basis upon which they rest.

It will appear very plain if we just think for a moment that such forms as Hooker tries to uphold are significant, or, in other words, are in themselves acts of worship: for since there is no scriptural authority for them, and since no act of worship sanctioned by the Scriptures requires them as necessary attendants, then they must either be meaningless and contrary to the light of nature, or if in accordance with the light of nature, significant, and therefore in themselves acts of worship, which worship is founded upon the precept of men, and is therefore will-worship, and may be shown to be sinful by the direct testimony of the Bible; for on this very point Christ says, "In vain do they worship me, teaching for doctrines the commandments of men,"* or rather He accepts the prophecy of Isaiah with approval, which says, "Their fear toward me is taught by the precept of men."†

2. The principle "whatever is not forbidden is permitted" still further tested in reference to the conduct of the Church as a worshipping Society.

Thus far we have endeavoured to explain our position in reference to the nature of the law regulating the worship of God, the worshipper being an individual; we shall next consider how it is, when the worshippers are united together as a society under a constitution and laws, with officers for the administration of such laws, as is the case in the Church.

But why, it may be asked, make this a matter for separate consideration? Because there is a marked difference between the regulating of our own conduct in accordance with what we think is right in worship, and the giving expression to the same in a law for the regulation of the conduct of others in worship. E. G., an individ-

---

* Matth. xv, 9.   † Is. xxix, 13.

ual learns from the Scriptures that he should pray, and that he may do so while standing, kneeling, or lying, or in fact in any position, or in a word, he has no direction as to the position except what the law of nature teaches him. Now the law of nature is that which speaks from his own heart to him, or in other words, it is the law of his common sense. He concludes that kneeling is the best position for him to take, and he is right in doing so; he would have been right too had he determined upon standing or some other position. But suppose this same individual to be a church officer laying down a law for the regulation of church members in reference to the same thing. He says, I myself, in a matter which is left to be decided by the laws of nature, have concluded that kneeling is the most becoming position, I therefore enact that all members of the church which I rule shall kneel at prayer. Is this individual then who was right, when he, out of several different positions (it being both by Scripture and the law of nature indifferent which position he took) chose kneeling, is he right now, we ask, when he enforces his own choice upon all who are under him? Certainly not; for while he had the liberty of choosing from several different positions, the one which suited him, he takes away the same liberty from others, and so adds a law of his own at variance both with Scripture and the law of nature. At variance with Scripture, because the Scripture by not enjoining a particular position allows liberty—at variance with Scripture, because he gives to that position an importance by making it binding upon all, which the Scriptures does not give to it; and at variance with the law of nature, because he teaches by *his* law, that that position is best, which nature says is no better than several others.

We say at once, that such power on the part of an individual is both arbitrary and tyrannical. But just suppose such an individual to be the mouth-piece of a synod, or the head of such a denomination as that of the Episcopal Church of England. You make a great mistake, some one exclaims, when you confound your supposed individual with a governing body. We do not think so at all. In every particular in which we draw a parallel, the cases are precisely the same. Let us compare the two. God has not given power to any individual to rule others in accordance with his own judgment of what is right; nor has He given such power to any governing body. It is arbitrary and tyrannical for any individual to impose the smallest burden which the Word of God does not warrant upon his fellows; it is also arbitrary and tyrannical for any governing body to do the same. Every individual governing others, must find a warrant for every law that he promulgates; every governing body must do the same.

Does not the State, it may be asked, enact many laws without a warrant from God. It may have done so, but it ought not to do so. But lest we be misunderstood, we shall here explain our position. The principles of natural justice are from God, and every law enacted by the State ought to be in accordance with these principles. If the laws are not, it is the duty of subjects to point it out, and it is the duty of rulers to bring their laws into conformity with these principles. This is the object for which all good rulers strive; and by so doing they acknowledge a standard higher than themselves. In the same way the Church, as a governing body, must find a warrant for every law which she promulgates.

So it does, says Hooker, but it does not find the warrant for all in the Bible, it gets its warrant for some from the laws of nature. We say it cannot find a warrant for those things which it enacts in accordance with the principle laid down by Hooker, which principle we have already quoted, either in the Bible or the law of nature. This statement we have already shown to be in accordance with fact by the illustration which we made use of a little way back. We saw at once that a thing which the law of nature may teach us, as individual worshippers, to be right, such as kneeling at prayer, must not be enforced upon others by an individual or by any governing body; and indeed it cannot be enacted by any governing body, without altering the case altogether as it stands under the law of nature. For the latter law teaches that we may sit, stand, kneel, or lie, while praying, *i.e.*, that we may take any position which we choose; but as soon as we turn from our own case, and legislate for others, it is entirely different. The law of nature says we may take any one of several positions; the legislator, according to our supposition, says you must kneel; which is a different law altogether, and deprives us at once of the liberty which the law of nature gives us. The law of nature says it is of no importance whether we stand, lie, kneel, or sit, while praying; the supposed legislator says, it is of so much importance that I will allow you only to kneel. In order then to have the people carry out the teaching of the Bible as far as it goes, and the law of nature where the Bible is silent, the legislator must not go beyond the warrant of the Bible in making any form obligatory. The contrary is Hooker's great mistake, the unsoundness, or rather part of the unsoundness of which, he challenges us to find in the principles which he took so much pains to work out. He shows us what we very well know, that in many things the law of nature is our only guide; but when claiming that the Church as a governing body may decree the observance of certain things, which are in accordance with the law of nature, and not contradictory to any precept of the Bible, he does not perceive that the decree of the governing body is not a law of nature at all, but another law, which, as we have already shown, does violence to the law of nature.

In what we have said concerning the position at prayer, be it remembered, we do not wish at the present time to establish any doctrine in reference to it. What we have said may be right or it may be wrong, we have only asked the reader to suppose it so for the sake of illustration. Let us now however by the principles which we have by that illustration wrought out, test some of those forms and ceremonies which Hooker thought he had so ably vindicated. The law of nature teaches me that under certain circumstances certain modes of dress are becoming. In the pulpit, for example, a black coat is becoming, or a black gown is becoming, or it may be that a white gown is becoming, or perhaps in other circumstances I could not do better than to wear a Chinese petticoat; but the liberty which the law of nature gives me is immediately snatched away, when I am made to comply with such a regulation as the following, "Such ornaments of the Church, and of the Ministers thereof, at all times of their ministration, shall be retained, and be in use, as were in this Church of *England*, by the authority of Parliament, in the Second Year of the Reign of King *Edward* the Sixth."* To take another example, I may think it quite proper under certain circumstances to dress my child in a particular way with certain ornaments, and as I myself am a member of the Church, I may take it, so dressed and ornamented, to the church to have it baptized; but when I am told that it must have in addition to the sign of the water, another sign applied to it, viz., that of the cross, I feel now that both the Scriptures and the law of nature are set at defiance. For let it be granted that there is no wrong whatever in applying the sign of the cross, then nature teaches me that I may disregard it, or observe it as I please; but the decree is, it must be observed; this I say is contrary to the law of nature. Further, the Scripture is violated. I know from the Scripture that I have a right to have my child baptized; but the decree is, you cannot have it baptized without the sign of the cross : thus the decree of man takes away what the Word of God gives.

We have now seen that everything enacted, and made obligatory on the members of the Church, in her polity, in addition to what the Bible warrants, violates both Scripture and the law of nature; hence we cannot lawfully have any form of Church Government except the Scrip-

---

* B. of C. Prayer.

tural form. We may now show in a positive way, instead of the negative, that we are bound to accept the Scriptural form.

I am told plainly in the Bible, that I must stand for myself at the last account—that I must give an account of myself to God. Under such circumstances, the law of nature teaches me, that *man* must not legislate for me in spiritual things. Whatever spiritual law I am to obey, must be one founded upon the authority of God, and that I must obey all the laws, and follow all the directions which He has given me, if I would seek the best interests of my own soul, as well as the salvation of the souls of others. But a certain one sends a particular man to be my minister, without asking my leave, or without consulting me in any way. I look into the Bible, and find that it is God's way that I should be consulted—in fact that I should have a say in the appointment of one to be my pastor. The law of nature also tells me, since I must give an account for myself, that I must, for myself, see to it that I have a pastor who can help me. I am bound too to do all I can for the spiritual welfare of my neighbours, and therefore I am bound to see that all inventions of men, which in any way abridge the spiritual liberty of myself or others, are resisted. In fine, as I must give an account of myself to God, and be judged in accordance with God's law, I must see to it that I carry out, and have carried out for me, in as far as I can, the precise laws which God has given. What holds true in reference to this particular part of Church Government, holds true in reference to every other part of it, and therefore, *The Scriptural form of Church Government* must be carried out, and no other form is of any authority; and this appears too both from Scripture and the law of nature.

Or it may be shown, that such is the case by any other example. I may be a minister called of God, accepted by His people, and set apart to the work of feeding the flock over which the Holy Ghost has made me a bishop. But certain ecclesiastical officers call me a priest, and say my duties are simply to preach, teach, and administer the sacraments. But in looking into my Bible, I find that I am, properly speaking, a bishop or elder, and that I am in conjunction with others, entitled to rule the people of God; in fact, that it is my duty to rule them; now as I must give an account of myself to God in accordance with what He requires of me, I must do this both for my own sake, and also for the sake of others; I must stand up for my privileges and duties. Where does the diocesan bishop get his authority over me? Not in the Bible, for that book knows nothing of such an officer. In the law of nature? No, for the exercise of the authority of such an officer violates the foundation principle of that law, which tells me that no man must come between me and my God, and prevent me performing my duty to Him. It appears then, both from the law of nature and Scripture, that the Scriptural form of Church Government must be carried out, and that no other is of any authority.

To sum up the results of this chapter, we have first, in reference to individuals regulating their own conduct, the following doctrines:—

a. Of the law regulating the worship of God this canon, WHATEVER IS NOT SANCTIONED IS PROHIBITED, *holds true.*

b. In case of worship's being performed by a significant form, such as the partaking of the Lord's Supper, or as in old times, the Feast of the Passover, *the above canon also holds true.*

c. In case of worship where no formal acts are specified, and only such implied as are necessary attendants, from the nature of things, upon the worship, as e. g., some one position or other in prayer, then the position or form may be such as the law of nature dictates.

We have secondly, in reference to a governing body acting in accordance with the constitution of the Church, and carrying out her laws, the following:—

a. Whatever liberty the individual has a right to by the Word of God and the law of nature, as related to that Word, must be preserved for him inviolate by that govern-

ing body. This necessitates the Church's leaving those things indifferent which are by nature indifferent, and at once confines her to the direct warrant of the Word of God for everything which she would bind upon her members.

b. It is her duty both to God and to her members, TO CARRY OUT ALL THOSE LAWS *which He has given for the regulation of His worship and service.* This makes it obligatory on ecclesiastical rulers to acquaint themselves with the teaching of the Scriptures, and in governing the Church, to conform to the same.

Under *a*, we have what cuts off all human systems of Church Government; under *b*, what secures the carrying out of the Scriptural Form.

THE END.

INDEX.

	PAGE.
Acts xiv. 23, critical examination of,	122
Alford on Bishop and Presbyter,	56, 73
Angels of the Seven Churches not Diocesans,	75
Apostles, extraordinary officers,	48
" qualifications of,	48
" as ordinary officers, were Elders,	59
Apostolical Succession,	21, 120
"Apt to teach," explained,	96
Bungener, quotations from,	135, 139
Campbell, Dr. P. C. on 1 Timothy v. 17,	93
" " on the Eldership,	87
Christ the Head of the Church in every sense,	128, 163
Christianity, its nature and place,	155
" different from morality,	156
" civil rulers not bound to teach it,	157
Church, what constitutes it,	11
" errors as to what constitutes it,	20
" its division into denominations unavoidable,	14
" of the Old Testament identical with that of the New,	28
" a visible form of the, necessary,	12

INDEX.

	PAGE.
Church, its members not to be expelled on suspicion,	13
" organization of the, as a society, necessary,	13
" existed before the day of Pentecost,	28
" of Judea, Galilee, and Samaria, under one government,	115
" Christ her Head in every sense,	128, 163
" how it teaches morality,	147, 159
" in what sense it seeks temporal ends,	150
Church Courts, proof for,	107
" a gradation of,	110
Church at Jerusalem governed by one court,	111
Church, officers of the, require qualifications different from those of the State,	152
Church and State, a sin to confound them,	153
" " distinct,	140
" " have different ends to gain.	146
" " have different constitutions,	151
" " various doctrines respecting,	140
Clergy and Laity, incorrect notions concerning,	118
Confession of Faith, what is it?	172
Constitutions of Church and State exactly suited to gain their respective ends,	148
Daillé, quotation from,	66
Deacons, their duties,	55, 99
Denominations, how accounted for,	15
Denominational differences, of how much importance,	16
" " advantage of discussing them,	19
Diaconate.	99
Diocesans not needed,	82
Diocesans, where it is thought an argument may be found in favour of,	58
Diversities of tongues have ceased,	53
Ecclesiastical power vested in the whole Church,	11, 120

INDEX.

	PAGE.
Elder and *Bishop* synonymous,	54
Elders and Deacons all the officers possessed by the Church,	54
Ellicott on Bishop and Presbyter,	58
Episcopalian arguments in favour of the three orders answered,	56
Errors in small things of great moment,	19
Evangelist, an extraordinary officer,	51
" his special work,	52
Extraordinary officers,	46
" " their qualifications,	46
" " distinguished from ordinary,	46
Gifts, what are the, now enjoyed by the Church,	42
Gifts of healing have ceased,	53
Gifted, treatment of, by the Presbyterian Church,	43
Governments,	84
" rule with the Elders,	85
Headship of Christ,	128
High Churchman, his errors as to the Church,	20
Hooker's principle contrary to both Scripture and the Law of Nature,	185–6–7
Hooker on the power of the Church,	174
Hooker, his admission in reference to the office of *Deacon*,	100
Independent, his objection to the doctrine of a Synod,	109
Jewish Hierarchy gives no support, to Prelacy,	77
Kelly on the Church criticised,	40
Macaulay, quotation from,	21
Magistrate, the civil, has no power in the Church,	140
Matthew xvi., 18, 19, critical examination of,	130
Matthias, case of,	49
M'Clure, quotation from,	69
Ministry, of what officers does it consist,	46

	PAGE.
Ministry, the,	32
" the Lord has given a, to the Church,	33
Offerings to God must be voluntary,	161
Office-bearers, appointment of,	118
Officers of the Church who have ceased,	47
Opinions of Episcopalians in reference to 1 Timothy v. 17,	91
" Independents " "	92
Ordain, to whom belongs the right to?	126
Ordinary officers distinguished from extraordinary,	46
" " who were they?	53
Ordination not necessary under all circumstances,	121
" what is it?	124
" its necessity,	125
Oxenden, quotations from,	17, 62
Papists' doctrine as to the Headship of Christ,	128
Pastor was a Presbyter,	53
Pastor and Teacher the same,	53
Pastors, Teachers, Helps, and Governments, known by other names,	53
Peter not the chief of the Apostles,	129
Plymouth Brethren, error of, with respect to the Church,	27
" " " " Ministry,	32
Pope not the Head of the Church,	129
Popular election, the right of the private members,	119
Prelatists' objection to the doctrine of an Assembly,	110
Presbyterian Church, theory of, respecting Governments,	91
Presbytery, proof for,	111
Prophet an extraordinary officer,	51
Protestant Church, in what sense she interprets,	170
Romanist, his error as to what constitutes the Church,	20, 164
Ruling Eldership,	86
" early history not contrary to,	89

Scriptural Form of Church Government, its Divine right,	174
Society, a, definition of,	141
State, expediency not the highest ground of,	150
,, how it teaches morality,	147, 158
,, man cannot submit to it in religion,	148
,, must not give up the Bible,	158
,, why it cannot use persuasion,	149
Stephen not necessarily a preacher,	100
Thesis, the,	9
Timothy's Diocese,	68
Timothy, Titus, and Epaphroditus, not Diocesans,	65
Titus, did he ordain alone?	72
Titus left in Crete,	71
Twelve and Seventy, case of, does not support Prelacy,	80
Unity, answer to the objection that there is none among Protestant denominations,	165
Various doctrines on Church and State,	140
Voluntaryism *versus* State support,	154
"Whatever is not forbidden is permitted," tested in reference to individuals when regulating their own conduct,	177
"Whatever is not forbidden is permitted," tested in reference to the Church when making laws for the regulation of the conduct of her members.	184

To Authors.

Jas. Campbell & Son,

Publishers of the Canadian Prize Sunday School Books, the National Series of Readers, and other School and Miscellaneous Books, are prepared to

FURNISH ESTIMATES TO AUTHORS

for the publication of their MSS., and may be consulted personally or by letter.

They will engage to have proofs carefully revised while passing through the press, if required.

The facilities possessed by Jas. Campbell & Son for the Publication of Books in the best Modern Styles, at the Lowest Prices, and their lengthened experience warrant them in undertaking the Publication of any work submitted to them, and in offering their services to Authors who desire to publish on their own account.

Toronto.

James Campbell & Son's Publications.

CANADIAN
Prize Sunday School Books.

KATIE JOHNSTONE'S CROSS,
A CANADIAN TALE.
By A. M. M.
Illustrated. 60 cts.

JESSIE GREY,
OR
THE DISCIPLINE OF LIFE,
A CANADIAN TALE.
By N. L. G.
Illustrated. 50 cts.

THE OLD AND THE NEW HOME,
A CANADIAN TALE.
By J. E.
Illustrated. 60 cts.

SOWING THE GOOD SEED,
By ALICIA.
A CANADIAN TALE.
Illustrated. 50 cts.

EMILY'S CHOICE,
A CANADIAN TALE.
By E. V. N.
Illustrated. 60 cts.

May be ordered of any Bookseller in the Dominion.